PRAISE FOR 1001 WAYS TO TAKE INITIATIVE AT WORK

"At last, a book that can actually raise your workplace IQ! *1001 Ways to Take Initiative at Work* is a comprehensive, yet practical guide to taking charge of your job, instead of letting your job take charge of you." *—Bob Rosner, nationally syndicated columnist and author of* Working Wounded: Advice That Adds Insult to Injury

"One of the critical competencies for employees at all levels of an organization is taking initiative. Read this book and learn how employees in organizations of all types and sizes have taken initiative to make a difference where they work and how you can, too." *—Patrick A. Dailey, Sr. Manager, Organization Learning, Nokia, Inc.*

"The power of employee initiative is not a myth. Bob Nelson captures the essence of what this movement can do for individuals and for an organization as a whole in his book *1001 Ways to Take Initiative at Work*. Employees know best how they can do their best work. In so doing, they become agents of their own change in improving their personal lives, their jobs, and their workplaces." *—Martin Edelston, President, Boardroom, Inc., Publishers of* Bottom Line/Business & Bottom Line/Personal *newsletters.*

"The success of any enterprise is predicated on the balancing of the needs of its constituents—customers, employees, owners/shareholders, strategic partners and community. Bob Nelson's book shows how employees who take the initiative to act in the best interests of the company and its constituents create value not only for their organization, but for themselves personally and professionally." *—Dieter H. Huckestein, Executive Vice President & President, Hotel Division, Hilton Hotels Corporation.*

"It's this simple: iVillage.com is the largest Internet site for women because every employee stepped forward with their ideas as if the success of the company depended on them. Because the truth is, the success of the company does depend on every person, whatever your position, whatever your department. It's wonderful to have a book, full of inspiration and how-to, which celebrates initiative as a win-win for employee and company alike. Loaded with examples, tools and action steps, *1001 Ways to Take Initiative at Work* is the resource for creating an even larger army of self-leaders that will drive any organization's success." *—Nancy Evans, President, iVillage.com*

BOOKS BY BOB NELSON

1001 Ways to Energize Employees
1001 Ways to Reward Employees
1001 Ways to Take Initiative at Work
365 Ways to Manage Better Page-A-Day® Perpetual
Motivating Today's Employees
Managing for Dummies
Consulting for Dummies
Empowering Employees Through Delegation
Delegation: The Power of Letting Go
Decision Point: A Business Game Book
Exploring the World of Business
The Perfect Letter
We Have to Start Meeting Like This: A Guide to Successful Meetings
Better Business Meetings
The Presentation Primer: Getting Your Point Across
Making More Effective Presentations
Louder and Funnier: A Practical Guide to Overcoming Stage Fright
The Supervisor's Guide to Controlling Absenteeism
The Job Hunt: The Biggest Job You'll Ever Have

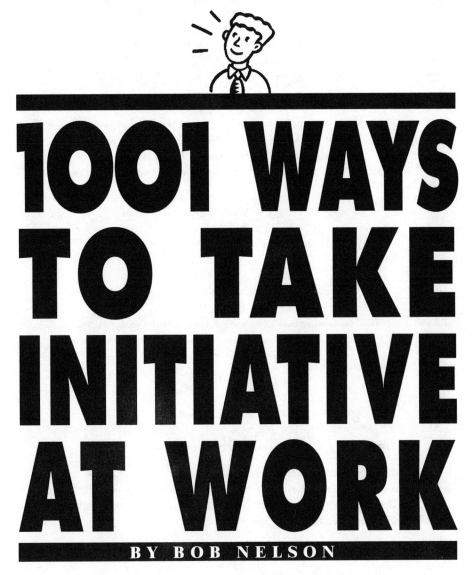

1001 WAYS TO TAKE INITIATIVE AT WORK

BY BOB NELSON

Illustrated by Matt Wawiorka

WORKMAN PUBLISHING, NEW YORK

Many thanks to iVillage.com for the use of
excerpts from their 1998 career poll.
Reprinted by permission of iVillage.com.

Published simultaneously in Canada by Thomas Allen & Son Limited.

Library of Congress Cataloging-in-Publication Data
Nelson, Bob, 1956–
1001 ways employees can take initiative / by Bob Nelson.
p. cm.
ISBN 0-7611-1405-X (alk. paper)
1. Leadership. 2. Employee motivation. 3. Industrial efficiency
1. Title.
II. Title: One thousand one ways employees can take initiative.
III. Title: One thousand and one ways employees can take initiative.
HD57.7.N446 1999
658.3'14—dc21 99-21940
CIP

Design by Lisa Hollander.
Cover illustrations by Burton Morris.
Interior illustrations by Matt Wawiorka.

Workman Publishing Company, Inc.
708 Broadway
New York, NY 10003-9555
www.workmanweb.com

First Printing September 1999
Manufactured in the United States
10 9 8 7 6 5 4 3 2 1

ACKNOWLEDGMENTS

It takes many people to make a book and many dedicated people to make a good book. I'd like to thank Peter Economy, business writer extradordinaire, researcher, and longtime friend, for his multi-year commitment to this project; Frank Kline, David Witt, and Rebecca Taff for their diligence in researching examples and clarifications; Sally Kovalchick, my gifted editor at Workman Publishing, and the many other tremendous individuals there who help create and distribute quality books, including Nettie Aljian, Laura Besserman, Peggy Boulos, Erin Cox, Katherine Detrich, Jeanne Emanuel, Andrea Glickson, Bruce Harris, Janet Harris, Lisa Hollander, Rena Kornbluh, Andrew Mandel, Jenny Mandel, Ellen Morgenstern, Jennifer Parmelee, Pat Upton, James Wehrle, and Peter and Carolan Workman; Lori Nunez for her typing assistance; and the hundreds of individuals who submitted items, responded to survey requests, or were interviewed for this book, including our Internet contest winner, Madelon S. Kuhn, who received $1,001 for her personal example of initiative *far* above and beyond the call of duty while an employee of 1-800-FLOWERS (featured on pages 142–144).

FOREWORD

The highest compliment one author can give another is: "I wish I had written that!" And that is exactly the compliment I gave Bob Nelson when I first read this book. In my own research, I have interviewed or surveyed thousands of managers on the topic of employee motivation. When asked what was the number one thing on their wish list for employees, they came back with the same resounding answer: "I wish my employees took more initiative." When I asked human resources managers what, in their minds, makes an outstanding employee, the overwhelming answer was initiative. And among the tens of thousands of employees I have surveyed over the years, nothing was more important or more motivating than to take initiative, and to then be recognized for doing so.

In my book *SuperMotivation,* I talk about "the greatest energy crisis in the world." This crisis is the enormous reservoir of human energy that exists in every human being, just waiting to be released—but that ends up being wasted because it was never used. Once lost, this energy is gone forever. The primary reasons for this "energy crisis" are not just a lack of initiative on the part of employees, but also managers who discourage, stifle, and even punish their employees for taking initiative.

I am convinced that the most successful organizations are the ones that actively encourage employees to take initiative, and the least successful ones are those that stifle initiative. Anyone can "go through the motions," but the behaviors that all organizations need in order to be successful require employee initiative. Creativity requires initiative. Outstanding customer service requires initiative. High quality requires initiative. In fact, virtually every organization was started by one or more people who took initiative to create a product, meet a need, serve a client, and organizations continue to thrive only if initiative continues.

Even so, I have heard just about every reason for employees not taking initiative: "It's not my job," "Nobody asked me to do that," "I don't want to rock the boat," and so on. Now there is no excuse for not taking initiative. Bob Nelson says, "Just do it!"—and he also provides the tools for doing it. This book is packed with ideas, examples, and resources that will take the risk out of taking initiative, and benefit the individual and the organization at the same time.

One more thing: Bob Nelson's books are not just meant to be read; they're also meant to be used. The next time you see something on the job that needs fixing, or a customer who needs your help, or a coworker who needs your support, take the initiative to make a difference—to make something happen. I guarantee that you will benefit by doing so, and so will your organization.

Dr. Dean Spitzer
Senior Consultant, IBM Corporation
Author of *SuperMotivation*

CONTENTS

PREFACE

The biggest mistake in life is to think that you work for someone else. True, you may have a boss and you may collect a paycheck from a company but, ultimately, you are master of your own destiny. You decide what potential you reach in your career and what you will eventually accomplish in your life.

Regardless of your circumstances, you *can* make a difference. This is particularly true at your current workplace. Every day you have the chance to excel, to stand out, and to be exceptional. You can make a suggestion to improve a product or service or to better serve your customers. You can identify an opportunity to save money or pursue a new idea or innovation. You can help a coworker do his or her job better or learn a new skill that you can use for the rest of your life.

It all comes down to initiative, that is, taking action to get something done at work without waiting for your boss to tell you what to do or when and how to do it.

This book is designed to help inspire and lead you on your journey. In it you will find many real-life examples that can encourage you to take charge, and practical tools and advice for helping you better yourself *and* the place where you work.

In this third book of the 1001 Ways series, which includes *1001 Ways to Reward Employees* and *1001 Ways to Energize Employees*, I want to get across the idea that all employees—not just managers—hold the keys to making a lasting and positive difference at work. As this book so amply illustrates, you can identify the things that need to be done and then act on them yourself. In most cases, not only will your manager be pleased that you have taken the initiative to get something done without being told, but your customers and clients will appreciate it as well.

I wish you all the best in improving yourself and your workplace. The power is within each and every one of you to make a difference. Now, seize the opportunity to do so!

—Bob Nelson
San Diego, California

On Taking Initiative

Whether he or she knows it or not,
every manager needs every employee
to participate and to speak up,
just as every employee
needs to be respected, trusted, and valued to
play a part in the big picture.
For no one person has all the answers
and no manager knows any job
as well as the person whose job it is,
nor should he or she even try to.
So commit to yourself,
right here and right now,
that you will never let an opportunity go by,
where improvement can be made,
or money saved,
or a customer better served,
without speaking up or making a suggestion.
For better or for worse,
it's your duty,
not only for your organization's benefit,
but for your own.
Dream big dreams,
and hold yourself to a higher standard.
Don't ever be afraid to say what's on your mind,
if you truly believe it will make things better.
You hold the key to your own future.
Make it the future *you* want it to be—
not the one someone else decides for you.

—B.N.

PART I

YOU AND YOUR JOB

Employees who make the personal decision to strive for something more than just the status quo are the lifeblood of every successful organization today. Taking initiative is a key ingredient in making improvements at work, dealing with change, and providing customers with service that is far beyond their expectations.

Initiative is personal: the individual controls when, where, and how much initiative to take on the job. Even though its impact may be felt throughout an organization, initiative starts with the employee—and what he or she can do on a daily basis.

In a recent online survey by iVillage.com, employees were asked, "What is most important for getting ahead in the workplace?" Of the 7,760 people who cast their votes, 55 percent said that "initiative" is most important, followed by "inspiration" (17 percent), "intelligence" (16 percent), and "political savvy" (12 percent). (Comments

about initiative taken from this survey are presented throughout this book.)

Although employees often recognize the importance of taking initiative, they may be hesitant to do so. Part I provides both ideas and inspiration for taking initiative on the job to overcome obstacles—real or perceived—that may be holding you back.

The chapters that follow provide a detailed overview of how *you* can take initiative, and in the process make a difference where you work. Whether it's tapping your inner creativity, taking needed action on a persistent problem, capitalizing on opportunities as they become available, or thinking up ways to improve your current work environment, the act of taking initiative will undoubtedly reenergize you, in addition to making your job much better and your organization more efficient and effective. By taking initiative, *all* employees can elevate their visibility within an organization and greatly improve their chances for recognition, learning, growth, pay raises, bonuses, and advancement for good performance.

By focusing on what you *can* rather than *can't* do, and emphasizing possibilities in your *own* sphere of influence, you'll increase your chances to not only have greater impact at work but develop your skills on a local basis before you apply them to a wider arena and obtain more lasting changes in your department, division, or organization.

Thinking Outsi the Box

Innovation is the spark that keeps organizations moving ever onward and upward. We innovate to (1) improve products and services, (2) find a new way to do something, (3) make a task easier or faster, (4) save money, (5) enhance our jobs, and (6) increase our promotability. Without innovation, new products, new services, and new ways of doing business would never emerge, and most organizations would be forever stuck doing the same old things the same old way. It has been said that 98 percent of an organization's problems can be solved routinely. However, the remaining 2 percent of an organization's problems—coincidentally, the problems that have the greatest effect on the organization—require employee innovation to surmount.

Despite the undeniably positive benefits of innovation within organizations, it seems that roadblocks to thinking creatively abound. According to a UCLA study, at age five, we engage in creative tasks 98 times a day, laugh 113 times, and ask questions 65 times. By the age of 44, however, the numbers shrink to 2 creative tasks a day, 11 laughs, and 6 questions. Furthermore, the UCLA study found a 91 percent *negative* response rate among adults exposed to new ideas. Creativity and innovation flourish in an environment that encourages them to grow and to blossom, but all it takes is a frown or a negative word to shut them down completely.

Think Differently

- Look for new combinations.
- Ask "what if?" or develop "what-if" scenarios.
- Consider approaches you've never thought about before.
- Brainstorm with others.
- Be a champion of new ideas—the old ways aren't always the best ways.

> “Initiative is the principal ingredient for success in the workplace.”
>
> —ANONYMOUS, from the Internet

Cheryl O'Connell, a senior buyer at United Electric Controls in Watertown, Massachusetts, noticed a workplace practice that directly affected her job. O'Connell became concerned that the company was storing many of its inexpensive labels in a very expensive stock-retrieval system. Buried beneath fasteners, springs, and stampings, the labels were hard to find—and often their adhesive had worn off by the time they were located. O'Connell would then have to order even more labels to replace the ones that were spoiled. After scavenging through existing company property, including a typing table and a four-sided corkboard, O'Connell and a coworker designed a special rack for the labels. It is, essentially, a pegboard on wheels, with rolls of labels hanging from the pegs. “We got a lot of ribbing,” she recalls. “You look at it and say, ‘It's not a rack and it's not shelving, so what is it?’” Nobody pokes fun anymore, though—especially those who remember what it was like to spend half an hour hunting down labels. “I don't work with labels, but when I think of things, I like to follow through,” says O'Connell. “Now I always find myself asking everybody, ‘Why do you do things that way?’ ”

While Brant Dolan, director of sales development for Marketing Innovators, an incentive and recognition products firm located in Chicago, Illinois, was on a family vacation in the Wisconsin Dells, he had his photo taken in a New York Yankees uniform, which was then superimposed on a *Sport* magazine cover by a company called Fotozines. Dolan thought, "What if I could offer this same experience to one of our clients' incentive winners for whom we were about to conduct a major incentive/recognition trip to Vail, Colorado?" Dolan had a hunch that they would get a kick out of seeing their faces on a cover of *Inc., Business Week,* or *Time* magazine.

Dolan took on the task of locating Fotozines and negotiating a fee for the company to come on site. He ran the idea by his client, USWest Communications, and they thought it was terrific. Ultimately, Dolan and his client chose *Skiing* magazine for the cover. When the winners arrived at Vail, they were told to report to the ballroom for a photo shoot, but they weren't told why. On the final day of the program, as the incentive winners entered the ballroom for a send-off breakfast, Dolan had arranged all of their photos—with their pictures on the cover of *Skiing* magazine—standing upright at more than 400 place settings. They were astonished, delighted, and amused, and they couldn't wait to get home to show their families. USWest was absolutely thrilled with the result of Dolan's initiative.

> "Thinking of yourself as self-employed is an attitude that says, 'I am a business partner; I have integrity and responsibility for working with the organization and the customer and for attending to my own personal and professional development.'"
>
> —Cliff Hakim, *We Are All Self-Employed*

One day, Rich Coutchie, an engineer at Lorin Industries, an anodized-aluminum products manufacturer in Muskegon, Michigan, was handling a 3.5-inch computer disc just like the millions of others in use around the world every day. He looked at the shutter door on the disk, which was then made of stainless steel,

The Scanlon Plan

Joseph Scanlon, a steelworker and union organizer during the 1940s and 1950s, noticed that when labor and management cooperated and employees were part of the decision-making process, companies tended to be healthier and workers more productive. He devised the Scanlon Plan based on the principles of "organization development, identity, participation, and equity."

Today, companies practicing the Scanlon tenets have joined to create Scanlon Plan Associates, a nonprofit organization that puts together annual conferences, publishes a newsletter, and serves as a clearinghouse for information on how to encourage employee involvement and other Scanlon initiatives. Visit them on the Internet at www.scanlonassociates.org.

and asked himself, "Why couldn't this shutter be made of anodized aluminum?" Good question. If it *could* be made of anodized aluminum, his idea would open up a huge new market for his company. And because Lorin Industries is a Scanlon participative management company—committed to the principles of identity, participation, equity, and competence—management listened to Coutchie's idea, and ultimately approved it. The impact of this idea for Lorin Industries included the building of an entirely new line to anodize the aluminum for this product and a 42 percent increase in sales.

Years ago, Spence Silver, a chemist at Minnesota Mining & Manufacturing (3M) in St. Paul, Minnesota, developed a strange adhesive. Instead of adhering strongly to the surfaces on which it was placed, this new adhesive barely stuck at all. After Silver made his discovery, many attempts were made by him and others within the company to find a use for this new "unsticky" adhesive—all to no avail. In the meantime, one of Silver's associates, 3M engineer Art Fry, was continually bothered by the problem of bookmarks falling out of his hymnal while he directed a church choir. This problem was quite annoying and Fry was committed to finding a solution. One day, as the frustrated choir director picked his bookmarks off the floor yet again, he thought of Silver's invention. By placing some of Silver's weak adhesive on the back of a piece of paper, Fry created a new kind of note—one that could be placed on an item, but easily removed when necessary without damaging either the note or the item on which it was placed. The product was initially distributed to administrative assistants internally at 3M. When they sought to reorder the note pads as they were depleted, the company knew they had a hit product. Today, Post-it® self-stick removable notes are a $300 million business.

> “Give it a try—and quick!”
>
> —Early 3M Motto

When Jenny Cutler, a programmer for a Silicon Valley firm, visited her mother-in-law in the hospital, she had a terrific idea for a new medical product that could be developed relatively easily by modifying one of her company's current products. Cutler asked both her boss and her boss's boss to meet with her about the idea. Impressed with Cutler's concept, they approved development of the new product, and she was authorized to spend up to half of her time developing a prototype and creating a financial forecast of its viability.

You just never know when or where a great idea for a new program or product will strike or what its ultimate effect will be on a company. For example, the name for Starbucks's innovative employee stock-option program—“Bean Stock”—was suggested by employee Bradley Honeycutt, who thought of the name one day while jogging with her husband. And in Santa Monica, California, Starbucks district manager Dina Campion pushed an idea for a

SEEING THE BIG PICTURE

To be able to take initiative in your job you first need to see how you and your position relate to the larger scheme of things at work. In most jobs this role is not explicitly explained, so you need to investigate how you fit into your organization's overall operation. Ask yourself:

Why was my job created? Most jobs are created to help with some pressing need of the organization: better or faster service, lower costs, fewer problems, improved opportunities. If you can understand the initial needs for your position, you will be better able to consistently address those needs—and go beyond them.

How does my job relate to others in the organization? Whom do you interact with every day? Whom do you support, and who are the people who support you? How can you make your manager's job easier? Questions like these help you to see the contribution you make in your position—and how you can expand it.

What opportunities to contribute to the organization exist in my job? Every job provides unique opportunities for the employee who looks for them. Consider the problems in your department. What part do you play in the process? What areas of operation do you get to observe? Knowing how you contribute to your organization can give you the leverage to do even more to help.

How is my job linked to the organization's objectives? By defining your position in terms of the goals and objectives of the organization, you can increase your worth to it. How does your position impact the mission of the organization? How does the customer benefit from the job you do? How does the organization make or save money based on your performance? Once you see your role in the big picture, you are better able to take the initiative to do those things that can best help.

frosty new coffee drink that she thought her customers would love—especially during those hot California summer days. Campion and a couple of other managers experimented with a variety of formulations until they got it just right. The ultimate concoction, dubbed "Frappuccino" (after a slushy coffee drink sold by Coffee Connection, the Boston coffee company Starbucks acquired in 1994), first became a local hit, and then took off nationwide, earning the company $100 million in its first year. Interestingly enough, Howard Schultz, chairman of Starbucks, didn't like the iced coffee drink at first: he thought it tasted "kind of froufrou." Schultz calls killing the Frappuccino idea the best mistake he never made, and he jokes that now he works for the woman who invented it. At Starbucks, employees are encouraged to innovate, and they are motivated by coworkers' examples.

> "Initiative is what companies thrive upon. If there is a problem, you want someone who will explore new theories and techniques without oversight. With someone who takes the initiative, intelligence follows through hard work."
>
> —Ken, from the Internet

In the super-competitive fast-food market, a little bit of creative initiative can go a long way toward building product sales. Danny Wagner, manager of a Kentucky Fried Chicken store in Boulder, Colorado, developed a $13.99 in-store meal special. What made this meal particularly special, apart from the fact that it consisted solely of highly profitable dark-meat pieces of chicken, was that every person who purchased the meal also received a chance to win a pair of tickets to a November 22 football game between the Oakland Raiders and the Denver Broncos. And by promising to advertise a local limousine service in his store for a week

before the drawing, Wagner was able to offer the lucky winner a free ride to the game and back home in style.

After seven years of running Tom & Sally's Handmade Chocolates, Inc., a gourmet chocolate business in Brattleboro, Vermont, Tom and Sally Fegley were talked into creating a new product—Chocolate Body Paint, a gooey confection that can be daubed onto loved ones—by a close friend and customer who first thought up the idea and then kept after them until they agreed to produce it. Although they initially resisted stocking the product in their staid store because they thought it might be a bit too suggestive, the friend persisted and Chocolate Body Paint was born. Today, the product is Tom and Sally's best seller, and it's won awards and been featured in publications from the *Wall Street Journal* to *Playboy* magazine.

Several years ago, when the office of Amy's Ice Creams in Austin, Texas, happened to run out of job application forms, a quick-thinking employee came up with an interesting way to reinvent the company's job application process. When all the applications were gone, the employee handed each remaining applicant an empty bag with instructions to do something creative with it. Because Amy's strives to hire people who can entertain customers, this brainstorm allowed applicants to demonstrate their

How to Be Creative on the Job

Kimberly Smithson, marketing manager of Motivation Online in Hoffman Estates, Illinois, offers the following tips:

- **Brainstorming.** The goal of brainstorming is to develop as many ideas as possible—not to critique, analyze, or discuss them or to make decisions. Create a chart and list as many ideas on a topic as possible. Some of the ideas may be pretty ridiculous, but everything goes on the list. The psychological principle behind brainstorming is called triggering. Any idea, no matter how dumb it seems, can trigger a viable idea.

- **Pare it down.** Most people think that in order to be creative, you have to invent something new. You can be just as creative by getting rid of things. By eliminating the unnecessary, you can improve

(continued on next page)

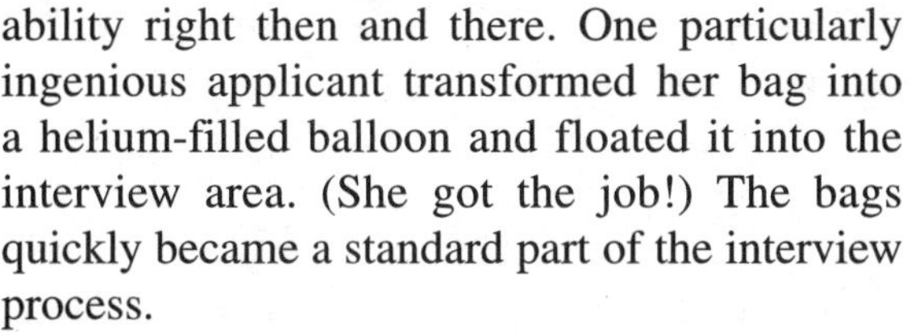

ability right then and there. One particularly ingenious applicant transformed her bag into a helium-filled balloon and floated it into the interview area. (She got the job!) The bags quickly became a standard part of the interview process.

Luis Catatao, an assembler of hermetically sealed switches at the Watertown, Massachusetts–based manufacturer United Electric Controls, found that he was constantly shuttling to the purchasing department to ask for more parts. Not only that, the company's computer wasn't always up to date: sometimes the parts he needed weren't even in the company's stockroom.

On his own initiative, Catatao began collecting information about the parts he used. How many had he used in the last three months? How did usage change over a six-month period? What was the lead time to get each part from the supplier? With numbers in hand, he approached production manager Harvey Chambers with his idea for a simpler way to track the parts. Using magnetic tabs, Catatao designed a board that indicates the status of inventory: a green arrow shows the current stock levels of all the parts he needs, and a red square sits at the reorder point for each part. As inventory shrinks, arrows close in on squares, threatening to gobble them in Pac-Man fashion. When arrows and squares drift dangerously close, parts need to be reordered. "Ever since I got this board, I run out much less than I used

(continued from previous page)

processes and ways of doing things.

- **Modify what exists.** By modifying something you already have, you may come up with something new, different, or better. You can also get a lot of good ideas by observing things around you. If you adapt what you observe in one context of your life, you may be able to solve a problem you face in another situation.
- **Lateral thinking.** Most of the time when you face a problem, you attack it logically—and that's good. However, what's logical may not be the only approach. Often the answer to a problem is not right in front of you, but can be found by looking at it from a different angle.

> “Initiative makes the difference between ‘robots at work’ and ‘people at work.’”
>
> —TOMAS(PR), from the Internet

to,” notes Catatao. “I can see where I stand in about two minutes.”

An employee of Gardner Merchant, a company in Kenley, Surrey, United Kingdom, that provides catering and food services to businesses and is now a part of the French-based Sodexho Alliance, came up with the idea of initiating a customer-profiling project. The worker suggested analyzing the social grouping of customers to pinpoint food tastes at each of Gardner Merchant's sites, which are mostly cafeterias that Gardner Merchant operates for its client companies. By serving at each restaurant the type of food that most closely matches the tastes of the main groups eating there, the company expects sales to improve significantly. And, in a bid to improve both product sales and the company's bottom line, staff at Gardner Merchant restaurants in Great Britain independently developed a “Food Miles” scheme to encourage more employees to eat on site. The program's adoption at British Steel in Corby, one of Gardner Merchant's clients, led to a 23 percent improvement in daily usage of the facilities. Cooking demonstrations at the Royal Insurance company cafeteria run by Gardner Merchant in Northern Ireland—another bright idea initiated by staff—led to a 12.5 percent increase in patronage.

Independent of management, engineers at Oregon Saw Chain (now the Oregon Cutting

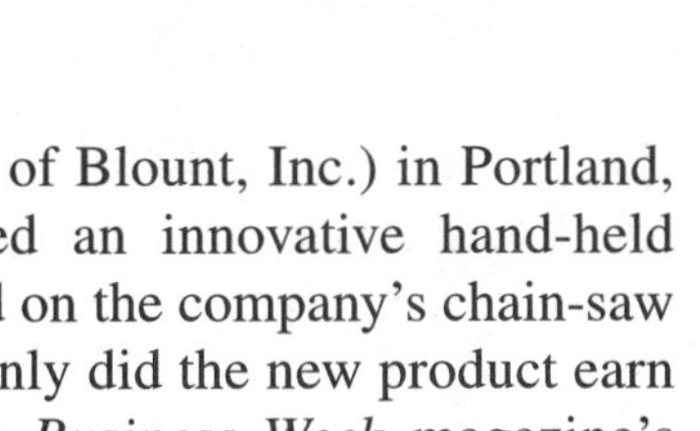

Systems Division of Blount, Inc.) in Portland, Oregon, developed an innovative hand-held pruning tool based on the company's chain-saw technology. Not only did the new product earn a silver medal in *Business Week* magazine's product-design competition, but it spawned a $5 million business unit that was ultimately sold off to another company.

At Going Places, Great Britain's second-largest travel agency, staff thought up the idea of compiling "Extra Mile" files to acquaint themselves and colleagues with particular travel destinations. This job aid, which includes personal observations on geography and local culture written by employees, helps all workers easily acquaint themselves with a variety of travel spots. Not only do the employees themselves benefit from knowing more about the destinations they are selling, but so do their clients.

Urged on by the possibility of improving the employee-compensation package, another group of workers at Going Places devised a unique performance-related pay scheme and successfully sold it to management. Its aim is to provide a way out of the low-pay, low-status, low-performance trap that is widespread in the travel industry. Maximum pay levels for "travel advisers" in shops will rise from approximately $14,000 to $28,000, says Tony Bennett, the managing director. "While we anticipate a 15 to 20 percent yearly increase in pay levels once the scheme is adopted, we are also delighted

“Initiative is taking the lead and never giving up regardless of what others do. The poem that I follow and taught my children says it all.

PRESS ON: Nothing in the world can take the place of persistence.

TALENT WILL NOT: Nothing is more common than unsuccessful men with talent.

GENIUS WILL NOT: Unrewarded genius is almost a proverb.

EDUCATION WILL NOT: The world is full of educated derelicts. Persistence and determination alone are omnipotent.

While I was never highly intelligent, I had initiative and persistence on any job I took. These qualities always brought great rewards and advancement to me (and my children as they went into jobs).”

—CJ,
from the Internet

Independent consultant Ken Tombs of Caterham, Surrey, United Kingdom, has established the following rules to guide his own efforts at creativity on the job:

- Maintain an open mind-set.
- Always learn from your mistakes.
- Be inquisitive (perhaps childishly so!).
- Keep asking why—even if you seem foolish in doing so.
- Don't suffer rubbish work gladly just because it exists.
- Read between the lines.
- Maintain a cynicism toward everything that seems "fashion or jargon oriented" and is not grounded in longer-term reality.

that this innovation by staff will actually pay for itself with a sales increase of the same magnitude," he says.

Loading sheets of steel into a forming press by hand is a very dangerous, labor-intensive, and expensive process. Two coworkers at Dana Corporation's plant in Elizabeth, Kentucky, were convinced that they could do something to improve the loading process. They figured out a way to automatically load steel sheets into a forming press, and then pitched their idea to management. The plant's management agreed and approved implementation of the project, which was a terrific success. As a result, six workers were reassigned to other jobs in the plant, saving the company $250,000 a year.

Jetway Systems in Ogden, Utah, manufactures the jetwalks used in boarding aircraft. The responsibility of Jerine Price's department is to manufacture all the electrical panels (consoles) that operate the jetwalk; the panels then move on to the final assembly area. Two years ago, the consoles were manufactured and delivered to the final assembly area without being pretested. As a result, many of them failed, and manufacture of the jetwalks was delayed up to 48 hours while workers troubleshot the consoles. Seeing a problem that needed to be solved, Jetway employee Dan Brown designed a console pretester on his own initiative for the department. The test device cost $1,000 to

UNLEASHING EMPLOYEE INNOVATION AND CREATIVITY

Just think how great it would be if all employees had the opportunity to contribute their ideas to their organizations and be appreciated for doing so. Fortunately, organizations today are increasingly relying on all workers, not just their managers, to find new creative ways to do business. According to Grace McGartlan, president of GM Consultants of Toronto, Ontario, anyone can unleash the untapped innovation and creativity in the workplace by applying the following principles:

1. Take the mystery out of creativity: define expected outcomes so that everyone in the organization understands where employees should direct their efforts.

2. Discover how individuals are creative: every person has his or her own approach to generating new ideas. Ask for input, but remember that people have different work styles.

3. Define challenges specifically: focus on areas where creative solutions are needed instead of wasting time on areas that generate little or no return to the individual or organization.

4. Minimize fear of failure: find ways to absorb risk. Regard mistakes as learning opportunities. Rewarding employees who take prudent risks will encourage them to innovate even more.

5. Take personal responsibility: develop an organizational climate for innovation. Start with yourself and the people within your personal sphere of influence.

6. Encourage active communications: set up hot lines among groups for quick, ongoing interactive idea exchanges.

7. Enhance your own creative skills and behavior: set an example.

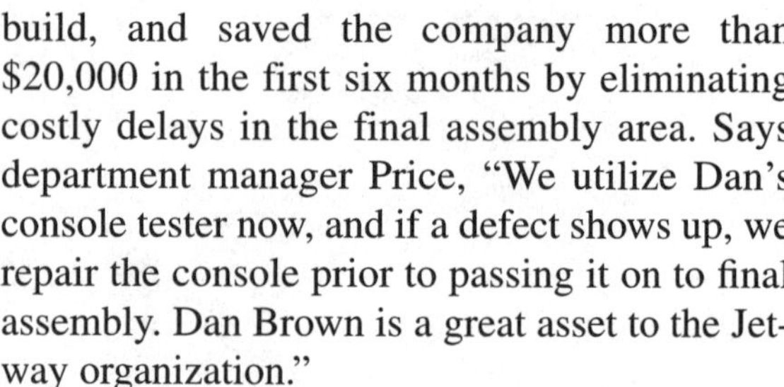

build, and saved the company more than $20,000 in the first six months by eliminating costly delays in the final assembly area. Says department manager Price, "We utilize Dan's console tester now, and if a defect shows up, we repair the console prior to passing it on to final assembly. Dan Brown is a great asset to the Jetway organization."

In an effort to help employees work better and more effectively with one another, many organizations give them personality assessments. Depending on how an employee answers a variety of questions, he or she is categorized into a specific personality type. After seeing how useful personality assessments can be in the workplace, Gail Seto, assistant manager of a Gap clothing store in Toronto, Ontario, developed a system of matching a salesperson's approach to a customer's personality type: for example, using a more intensive approach when a customer clearly needs some help in deciding what to buy. Gail pitched the idea to her regional manager, who liked it and asked her to present her "Knowing Your Customer" system to all district managers so that they could take it back to their stores and train their own employees.

Initiative is also important in small-group settings. Lois Frankel attended a professional association meeting whose topic was team building. The speaker broke the participants

The Right Stuff

Ravi Kapur at the Naval Research lab in Washington, D.C., offers the following traits that are important to anyone who wants to take initiative:

1. Strong belief in your principles
2. Ability to challenge the status quo
3. Ability to see what we all see, differently
4. Degree of selflessness

into groups and asked them to use a stack of newspapers, masking tape, and scissors to build the tallest tree that they could. Lois, who is used to thinking creatively, looked up at the ceiling and saw that it was recessed (it was lower in the areas where the groups were assigned to work) and suggested to her group that they first move to the center of the room, where the ceiling was higher, so that they could build a taller tree. Then she suggested that they cover a table with newspaper and build the tree on top of it. Several members of Lois's group were reluctant to use anything other than the material provided and to move out of the designated area. The other people in Lois's group were all

> "You can have all the skills and talents in the world but without the initiative to apply them they do no good."
>
> —ANONYMOUS, from the Internet

PERSONAL ATTRIBUTES FOR INITIATIVE

TAKE ACTION NOW!

1. Take time to be creative. Schedule a regular appointment with yourself to think about the big picture and new ways to solve old problems.

2. Be open to new ideas. Listen to your coworkers, encourage their creativity, and respect their opinions.

3. Put your ideas into action. Coming up with an idea is only part of the equation. Ideas are worthless if you do not follow through.

4. Be persistent. Not everyone is going to agree with your ideas, and even if they do, it may take some time to bring them around to your way of thinking.

5. Take risks. The biggest organizational payoffs occur in an environment where risk taking is encouraged.

> “Make every decision as if you owned the whole company.”
>
> —Robert Townsend, Former CEO, Avis

employees—she was the only consultant—and their reluctance stemmed from working in organizations where creativity and initiative were not encouraged or fostered. Lois persisted, however, and the team broke out of its narrow thinking and won the competition.

Doing Your Homework

As many prosperous businesspeople already know, preparation is often the key to success in any endeavor. You may be socially adept at work and have a pleasant enough personality, but you'll be more likely to convince others that your solution is the right one if you have the facts on your side. Doing your homework means taking the initiative to be prepared for any challenge: making a presentation, participating in a meeting, advancing a new idea to your boss, or overhauling company processes and procedures. And doing your homework also means doing the basic research necessary to back up whatever claims you are making: new ways to cut costs, improve product development, or better gauge the effect of your organization's policies and practices on your customers.

J. Douglas Phillips, senior director of corporate planning at Merck headquarters in White House Station, New Jersey, takes the innovative step of using cost studies of employee turnover to justify the company's investments in work and family benefits. The research he does before he presents his proposals to management pays off in a big way. According to Phillips, such bottom-line demonstrations add to his internal credibility in promoting such programs as day-care centers and lunchtime employee forums on teenage drug abuse.

Be prepared

- Get background on the situation.
- Think through the problem or issue.
- Do a cost-benefit analysis.
- Anticipate additional needs.
- Bounce your thinking off your boss or a colleague.

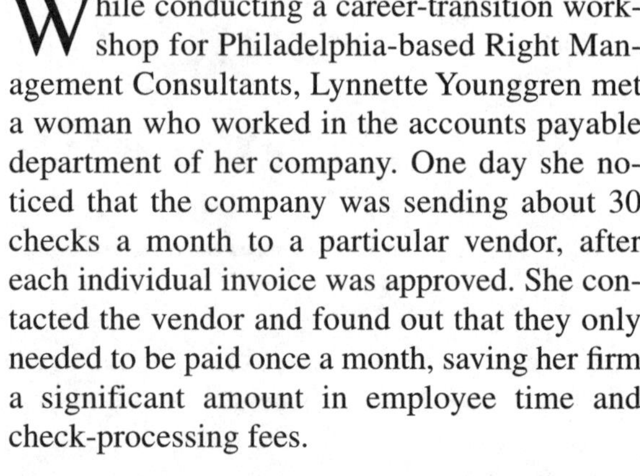

While conducting a career-transition workshop for Philadelphia-based Right Management Consultants, Lynnette Younggren met a woman who worked in the accounts payable department of her company. One day she noticed that the company was sending about 30 checks a month to a particular vendor, after each individual invoice was approved. She contacted the vendor and found out that they only needed to be paid once a month, saving her firm a significant amount in employee time and check-processing fees.

> "All progress is made in defiance of management."
>
> —Bob Woodward, Reporter, *The Washington Post*

When Patrick Sinner at PNC Bank of Pittsburgh, Pennsylvania, came up with the energy-saving idea of requiring employees to turn off their computers at the end of each workday, management demurred, citing a commonly held but erroneous belief that regularly switching the computer on and off would dramatically shorten its life. However, Sinner didn't quit there. He further researched the topic and came up with research studies that supported his belief. When Sinner presented these studies to management, thus proving that the computers would be retired long before any negative impact of all the on-and-off switching would show on the equipment, management finally agreed. The resulting energy savings amounted to $268,000 per year.

Before flying to California to interview for a job as Midwest regional sales manager for

LEARN FROM YOUR MISTAKES

We all make mistakes at work; however, we all don't learn from our mistakes. To avoid repeating your errors, you need to identify, learn from, and apply your learning to future situations.

Be able to identify your mistakes. This may seem obvious, but many people don't learn from their mistakes because they don't see them as errors to begin with. For example, a coworker gets mad at you for not informing him of a parts backlog that affects his job. You get defensive and explain that it's not your job to tell him. Do you learn from the situation and try to prevent it from happening again, or do you dismiss the situation as "his problem"? Define a mistake as "when something didn't happen the way you expected," or "when you were unexpectedly surprised in an unpleasant way." This way of identifying mistakes allows you to watch for a larger set of potential problems that affect you, your job, or the relationships you have with others at work so that you can prevent negative situations before they occur.

Ask yourself (and others) what could have been done differently. Even if the problem was not your fault, take the initiative and assume responsibility for finding a solution that will make your job—and the job of your coworkers—easier in the future. Seek feedback from others affected by the problem or from your manager or coworkers. If they weren't involved with the problem, explain the situation and ask their opinion on what they would have done. Explore possible scenarios for prevention with them.

Plan to apply what you learned in future situations. Be proactive in preventing the same or a related mistake. Tell others about your plans, especially if they might be affected.

> “What differentiates one from his or her colleagues with the same academic background is the ability to use initiative to project one’s self as most suitable for a given position.”
>
> —PATRICIA SHIPLEY, from the Internet

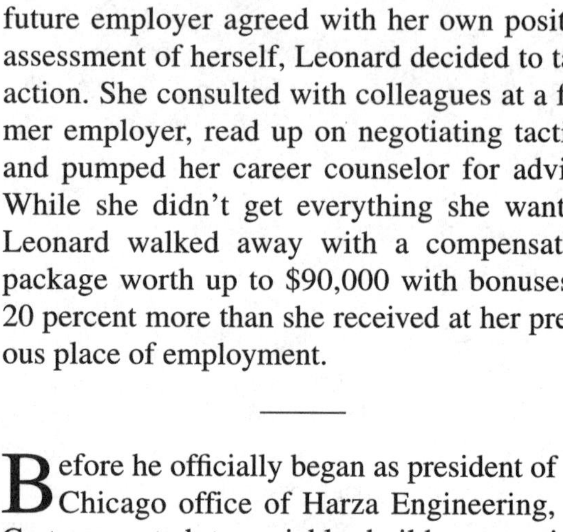

the Trefethen Winery in Napa, Cindy Leonard knew that to get the job and adequate compensation she would have to stand head and shoulders above her competition. To make sure her future employer agreed with her own positive assessment of herself, Leonard decided to take action. She consulted with colleagues at a former employer, read up on negotiating tactics, and pumped her career counselor for advice. While she didn’t get everything she wanted, Leonard walked away with a compensation package worth up to $90,000 with bonuses—20 percent more than she received at her previous place of employment.

Before he officially began as president of the Chicago office of Harza Engineering, Ed Carter wanted to quickly build connections with his new staff. To achieve this goal, Carter proactively developed a way to meet the company’s employees far more quickly than if he simply met them during the normal course of business. He asked 30 top employees to complete a detailed survey that served as a basis for an in-depth, 90-minute one-on-one discussion. He also scheduled weekly lunches with all 140 other staff members, ten employees at a time, effectively getting to know them and forging associations with every employee in less than 12 weeks.

Kelly McGovern, former vice president of Internet/telecommunications at Bay Net-

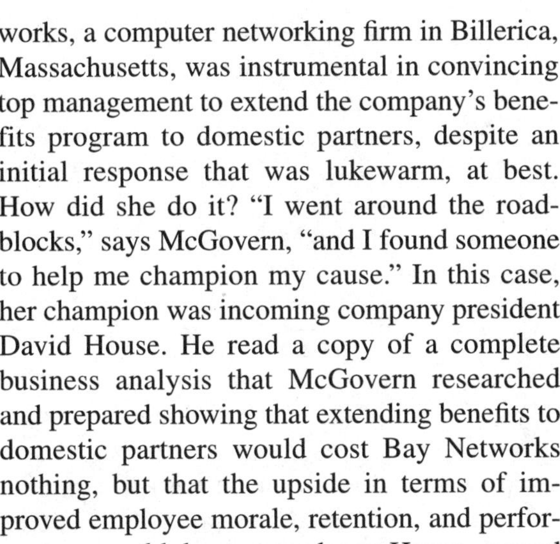

works, a computer networking firm in Billerica, Massachusetts, was instrumental in convincing top management to extend the company's benefits program to domestic partners, despite an initial response that was lukewarm, at best. How did she do it? "I went around the roadblocks," says McGovern, "and I found someone to help me champion my cause." In this case, her champion was incoming company president David House. He read a copy of a complete business analysis that McGovern researched and prepared showing that extending benefits to domestic partners would cost Bay Networks nothing, but that the upside in terms of improved employee morale, retention, and performance would be tremendous. House agreed with her analysis, and the program was immediately put into effect.

> “It is better to solve problems than crises.”
>
> —JOHN GUINTHER, American Writer

Few salespeople take the time to thoroughly research their prospects and their unique needs and operating environments. However, Jeremy Barbera knows that taking the time and initiative to learn a bit about his potential clients before he meets with them can go a very long way in helping to make a sale, and to satisfy his clients' needs at the same time. Barbera, founder and CEO of Marketing Services Group in New York City, helps clients design databases and implement direct-mail campaigns to attract new customers. After he sets up an appointment to see a new prospect—typically orchestras or museums—Barbera researches the organization extensively to discover its

specific marketing problems, then devises a solution to present at the first meeting. In most cases, his prospects, who expect to spend the first meeting simply explaining their problems, are pleasantly surprised that Barbera not only knows what their problems are, but has already thought about ways to solve them.

"Recently I volunteered to help with the company picnic. I organized the games and activities for the day. I feel as though I was a good example to others by taking the initiative to help. The picnic was a success and I feel a sense of accomplishment and satisfaction."

—Melissa Fightmaster, University Liaison, WYNCOM

Refrigeration and air-conditioning manufacturer Copeland Corporation of Sidney, Ohio, was having problems with a particular drill bit. Performance was poor and it sometimes broke off in the product; yet the bit cost only $4.50, which seemed economical to management. A self-managed team of drill operators at the plant was certain that using a higher-quality bit would be more cost effective in the long run, so some of the team members researched more expensive drill bits while others collected data on the bit they were using. They were able to provide management with data showing that a bit costing twice as much would last three times as long, thereby reducing damaged goods and machine downtime. Copeland makes it a practice to recognize such initiative monthly at both of its refrigeration and air-conditioning plants, according to plant manager Gerry Ulrich.

For years, environmental activists who objected vocally to the elaborate styrene foam containers that McDonald's, the fast-food chain headquartered in Oak Brook, Illinois, used to package its sandwiches caused the company much grief. Convinced that it was doing the right thing, by providing its customers with the

SYSTEMATIC PROBLEM SOLVING

Solving problems is often the reason why many employees take initiative in the first place. Here are some suggestions for solving problems in a systematic way:

1. Define the problem. Is there really a problem? If so, determine exactly what it is, how big it is, and if it is going to continue to be a problem in the future.

2. Gather data. Before you start looking for solutions to the problem, gather as much data about it as you possibly can without unduly delaying your efforts.

3. Consider alternate solutions to the problem. Make a list of the most likely solutions to the problem and prioritize them from most to least likely.

4. Pick the best solution. Choose the most likely solution at the top of your list. Be ready to proceed to the next solution if your first choice does not generate the results you seek.

5. Apply the best solution. Put your most likely solution into action. Closely monitor the results to see if it solves your problem. If so, congratulations! You can move on to the next problem. If not, apply the next most likely solution.

> “New ideas . . . are not born in a conforming environment.”
>
> —Roger von Oech, President, Creative Think, Inc.

highest-quality product, McDonald's management found itself at odds with the people who demanded that the fast-food maker package its products in more ecologically friendly materials, such as paper and cardboard. When it seemed that both sides had reached an impasse, a mid-level employee at McDonald's took the initiative to pull together information showing how different packaging could not only save the company money but also put McDonald's on the forefront of the increasingly popular environmental movement. Management liked what it saw, and accepted the employee's plan overwhelmingly.

Kathleen Betts, a mother of two who shared her job working for the Massachusetts state government with another mom, was concerned about her job security when Governor William Weld announced his vow to lay off hundreds of state workers and to furlough others in a bid to balance the state's budget, which was $460 million in the red. Using only her personal time away from the office, Betts researched the state's Medicaid rules and federal Department of Human Services guidelines in hopes of finding a way to generate a few more dollars here or there. Her initiative, as well as her extensive research, uncovered an accounting wrinkle that entitled the state to get reimbursed at a much higher rate than it had been—to the tune of $489 million. Not only was the budget gap immediately closed, but

there was $29 million to spare. Betts received a cash award of $10,000 for her initiative and work, as well as thanks from a very grateful Governor Weld.

IDENTIFYING YOUR ORGANIZATION'S CULTURE, VALUES, AND NORMS

TAKE ACTION NOW!

In business, doing your homework means many different things, from learning everything you can about possible options or alternatives before you make a decision, to being prepared for meetings and presentations. One especially critical factor to consider is the culture of the organization you work for: each organization has its own set of values and norms—the ideals that are held in high esteem by management and used as models for good employee behavior. For your initiatives to be successful, you have to tailor your approach accordingly.

1. Research your organization's culture by talking with your colleagues—both workers and managers—about what norms, values, and beliefs are most important to your organization and to the individuals who work within it.

2. Map out your organization's decision-making channels and take time to get to know each person in the channels you wish to influence.

3. Seek out and develop informal channels for influencing others in your organization, in a way consistent with the organization's culture.

4. Cultivate networks of coworkers who can support you in your efforts and influence others on your behalf.

5. As you prepare to influence others in your organization, be sure that your anticipated approach is consistent with the organization's culture.

Taking Action/ Capitalizing on Opportunities

In any business situation, there comes a time to bring to a close deliberations, discussions, and analysis, and to take action. If you're not officially cast in a management role of your organization, taking independent action can be a scary proposition—after all, it would be much easier to wait for your boss to not only make the decision but to take responsibility for it as well. However, today's organizations cannot afford to employ workers who simply wait to be told what to do. If your business is to thrive in the coming years, it needs workers who are willing not only to take chances and to make decisions but also to take actions and responsibility for their actions. Fortunately, most managers welcome such initiative, and they are increasingly willing to give their employees more responsibility, autonomy, and authority in their jobs.

> "If you have initiative, you don't need someone telling you what to do all the time."
>
> —Frank, from the Internet

A government agency in New Zealand printed a number of brochures with an incorrect toll-free phone number and distributed them throughout the country. The result was a flood of confused calls to CLEAR Communications, the owner of the incorrect phone number. While management was busily telling the company's receptionists how to refer callers to the correct number, a bright sales agent at CLEAR spotted

an opportunity. He called the government agency and sold them the incorrect phone number! He not only solved the problems of the government agency and CLEAR's busy receptionists but generated a sale for himself as well.

Fastenal, a supplier of nuts, bolts, and other fasteners based in Winona, Minnesota, can charge a premium price for its products because its employees make a point of satisfying the customer and capitalizing on opportunities as they arise. When Machinery Services Corporation, a client in Paterson, New Jersey, ran out of stainless-steel U-bolts, Fastenal's Hackensack, New Jersey, branch manager Keith Greaves sprung into action. Recalls Greaves, "They weren't in stock, and none were coming in the next day. I drove to the hub in Scranton, Pennsylvania, at 2:00 A.M. to get them." So Machinery Services had its U-bolts in hand by 6:30 A.M. for a price of $8 each, about 75 cents more than the price charged by Fastenal's rivals.

For years, Johnsonville Foods, a sausage maker in Sheboygan, Wisconsin, sold its products only in the Midwest. This created quite a problem for people who moved out of the area, leaving their favorite brand of bratwurst behind. For secretary Elaine Crawford, however, this problem represented an opportunity for the company—one that could be addressed with just a little bit of initiative and an investment of time on her part. She seized on

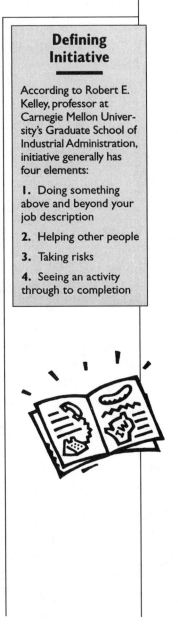

Defining Initiative

According to Robert E. Kelley, professor at Carnegie Mellon University's Graduate School of Industrial Administration, initiative generally has four elements:

1. Doing something above and beyond your job description
2. Helping other people
3. Taking risks
4. Seeing an activity through to completion

TAKING RESPONSIBILITY FOR YOUR ACTIONS

BE YOUR OWN BOSS

We're all responsible for our own actions. This fundamental belief is the foundation for all individuals who take initiative and are in control of their lives. You can be a victim of your circumstances—complaining, feeling sorry for yourself, and believing that life is unfair—or you can rise above the negative elements of the current circumstances, be accountable for your actions, and focus on what can be done to improve or correct the situation. Here are some tips for taking responsibility for your actions:

Do what you say you'll do. Be a person of your word. Complete tasks in a timely fashion. Don't rely on others to remind you of your commitments, and don't wait to begin a task until it is due. Have a system for staying on top of your commitments, and take the steps necessary to assure successful completion. If you can't fulfill a commitment, tell others prior to the deadline, or seek help to meet your schedule. Finish what you agree to take on.

Own up when you have made a mistake. If you blame another person, a system, or an event for something you did wrong, others will not trust you. Don't participate in the "blame game," even if coworkers play it. People will think more of you (and more quickly forgive you) if you are quick to claim a mistake you made and are eager to focus on a solution to the existing situation. They will be suspicious of you and your intentions if you deny responsibility that turns out to be yours, and as a consequence may distrust what you say or avoid working with you.

Don't make excuses for yourself or for others. Deliver what you promise and expect others to do the same. Always strive to do your best and expect the best from others. If there is a problem, find out why it occurred and use the facts to develop a solution. Be responsive when following up on problems—especially with customers. Don't accept low-quality work from yourself or others. Don't rationalize.

the idea that the company should offer its products by mail order and presented it to her boss. He assigned her the task of writing up a business plan for such an operation. Management approved the plan and Crawford was put in charge of the mail-order department, which became a significant source of revenue for the company.

Harry Allen, sanitation and fleet services manager for the city of Longview, Texas, refuses to get caught up in the bureaucratic red tape that hamstrings many public entities. Allen realized that employees work better and more effectively when they are allowed to go home after their jobs are done for the day. He therefore decided to put his sanitation haulers on a task basis, where they were assigned certain tasks to accomplish each day. So while other city staffers work 40-hour weeks—whether they have caught up with their work or not—sanitation truck drivers and trash collectors work on a task basis. When they finish their prescribed work for the day, they are free to go. Although his approach creates no end of headaches for the city's administrative staff, Allen's workers consistently maintain the best customer service numbers in the city, as well as the best employee morale.

As a part-time transfer coordinator for Children's Medical Center of Dallas, Texas, and a full-time paramedic and firefighter for the city

Be Proactive, Not Reactive

- Do it now!
- Make a list of the excuses you use to avoid taking action on the job. Review it closely and vow not to use these excuses again.
- Trust your intuition—and act on it.
- Asking for forgiveness is easier than asking for permission. If you know what needs to be done, do it now and explain yourself later.
- Learn to balance your duty to obey with your duty to disobey when something is clearly wrong.

> “If you do it right 51 percent of the time you will end up a hero.”
>
> —ALFRED P. SLOAN, Former President and Chairman, General Motors

of Carrollton, Texas, Ken Frederickson was concerned that Children's was not included as an accepted medical center in his employee health insurance plan from the city of Carrollton. Says Frederickson, "I work at Children's, and my wife is a nurse at Children's, and we believe that this is where the best care is. If we needed to use its facilities, we wanted it covered under our health insurance plan." When he learned that the city was making changes to its employee health benefits program, Frederickson acted quickly and

A WORKING CREED FOR TAKING THE INITIATIVE

Cliff Hakim, founder of Rethinking Work, a consultancy specializing in individual and organizational change and renewal, presents the following Working Creed, which any employee should consider as he or she prepares to take initiative:

I will begin the process of change with myself.
Start with my own personal growth.
I will face the dragon—my work fears.
Replace fear with passion.
I will integrate independence and interdependence.
Be myself and collaborate with others.
I will join, not work for, my organization and customers.
Build work and work relationships based on equality and competence.
I will commit to continuous learning.
View my career as a lifetime endeavor.
I will create meaningful work.
Work, believing that the world offers what I need and that I can make a contribution.

contacted Sally Lyon, Children's director of market development. Lyon got the ball rolling to have Children's Medical Center included in the city of Carrollton's employee health network. Says Lyon, "Ken went above and beyond the call of duty and we're appreciative of his effort to ensure that all children have access to Children's."

When news spread that US Airways planned to shut down its maintenance operations in Winston-Salem, North Carolina—laying off 1,300 workers in the process—employees decided to take action. On their own initiative, a group of US Airways workers developed and presented an alternate proposal to management—one that would easily consolidate the maintenance operations from other parts of the country in one place and bring more than 300 workers to Winston-Salem.

According to Don Harrison, public relations manager for Home Depot, based in Atlanta, Georgia, personnel in both Oklahoma City stores reacted immediately in 1995 when they heard that the Federal Building had been bombed. According to Harrison, both store managers, independently and on their own initiative, cleaned out their stock of plywood, tarps, and timbers and loaded their delivery trucks to rush to the assistance of those on-site, without getting approval from—or even notifying—company headquarters.

Setting Goals

To get things done it's important to set goals, but what is the difference between a good goal and one that misses the mark? The best goals are:

- Few in number, specific in focus
- Not too hard, not too easy
- Mutually agreed upon, with others who will work toward the goal
- Visualized and written down

And when it comes to deciding exactly what goals to focus on, ask yourself these questions:

- What actions give you the greatest impact?
- What one thing will you do differently? How will you keep your commitment to doing that one thing?

Do What Has to Be Done

When it comes to taking initiative on the job, Dwight Jones, storekeeper at the San Diego Housing Commission in San Diego, California, is a model employee. Years of outstanding performance reviews by his supervisor, along with a variety of organizational and departmental rewards and recognition bear this out.

Why take initiative? According to Jones, "Most employers—probably 99.9 percent of them—prefer not to have employees who constantly have to be told what to do. To me, it's common sense—if there's something there that needs to be done, you should take the initiative to go do it, and not wait until someone comes up to tell you that you need to do it."

Jones clearly derives a lot of personal and organizational pride from taking action instead of waiting for someone to tell him what to do. Says Jones, "I think initiative comes

(continued on next page)

When it comes to business, Jay Goltz, author of *The Street-Smart Entrepreneur,* has nothing to prove. As founder and president of Artists' Frame Service in Chicago, Illinois, Goltz built a $2,000 investment into a $9 million custom-framing facility, one of the largest in the world. When Goltz had the opportunity to buy the building next door to his thriving framing operation, he jumped at it. After buying the property, the next question was what to do with it. The result is Jayson Home & Garden, a florist and retail garden center. Although Goltz didn't know anything at all about the industry, he has produced another winner. Jayson Home & Garden is Chicago's hottest florist and garden center. According to Goltz, the fact that he didn't know anything about running a plant store was actually a benefit. "Since I didn't know anything about the business, I hired the most talented gardening people I could find, and then left them alone to run things."

Al Billings, water distribution supervisor for the city of Chandler, Arizona, was faced with implementing a host of new safety orders to protect his crews who worked with chlorine gas every day within a very limited budget. "Basically, I was looking for a way to handle the chlorine, which would make it safer for the guys," said Billings, who tackled the problem by inventing a way to use solid chlorine in the city's system instead of chlorine gas. Billings and his crews, with the help of water systems coworkers

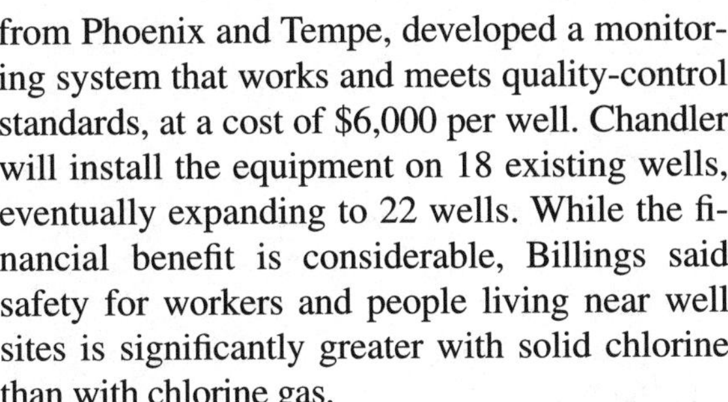

from Phoenix and Tempe, developed a monitoring system that works and meets quality-control standards, at a cost of $6,000 per well. Chandler will install the equipment on 18 existing wells, eventually expanding to 22 wells. While the financial benefit is considerable, Billings said safety for workers and people living near well sites is significantly greater with solid chlorine than with chlorine gas.

A number of brand names are so popular that it's difficult to imagine a time when they struggled for recognition. However, many years ago, the Clorox Company of Oakland, California, which has annual sales of $2.7 billion, was a young start-up venture that could barely afford to pay its employees. At least that was the case until Annie Murray, wife of an original investor in the Clorox Company and proprietress of the family's grocery store, decided to try a new approach to jump-starting sales of the company's bleach. Her idea was to give her customers free samples of a diluted version of the commercial bleach that the company produced for home use. Impressed by the results of Murray's giveaways—she was receiving inquiries and requests for the product from as far away as the East Coast and Canada—the company adopted her tactic as a primary marketing tool. The product soon became popular as a laundry aid and disinfectant, and the Clorox Company, which had been on the verge of bankruptcy, quickly became a huge success.

(continued from previous page)

from within. It's seeing something that needs to be done and just taking care of it. For me it's a personal satisfaction to see how far I can push myself and to see how much I can get done within a day. I finish one project and then I'll go on to the next to see if I can get it done. When you go above and beyond your normal duties and complete a project sooner than your boss expected you to, it feels *great.*"

Several years ago, Karen Edwards worked in the customer service department of a small company in Virginia named Quantum Computer Services. One day, Edwards heard Quantum's CEO describe how he wanted to add a human voice to the company's computer user interface. Recognizing an opportunity, Edwards immediately thought of her husband Elwood, who had worked in local radio and television for a number of years. "Hey, you ought to try Elwood," she suggested. "He'd be great!" The CEO agreed to give Elwood a try and he recorded four simple phrases on a tape recorder: "Welcome," "You've Got Mail," "File's Done," and "Goodbye." Soon after Elwood made the recordings, Quantum changed its name to America Online, and today millions of people hear his voice every time they log onto the network.

At Oticon, a hearing aid manufacturer headquartered in Hellerup, Denmark, employees routinely volunteer for tasks, projects, and teams throughout the company. The network that has developed from these individual employee initiatives has effectively replaced the company's standard management and bureaucracy. For example, secretary Inge Christophersen saw a need for advanced word processing training in her organization. After polling her coworkers and finding that a number of employees were indeed interested in attending, she organized a class and became the instructor—all on her own initiative and

ATTITUDE AND BALANCE ARE IMPORTANT TO TAKING ACTION

TOOL BOX

We all know that we should take better care of ourselves, relax more, and have more fun at work (and elsewhere, as well!), but it's easy to overlook the opportunities to do just that because of the daily work priorities that consume our lives. Here are some ideas for learning to take action in your own work life:

- **Get healthy.** Regular exercise will not only make your mind and body stronger but also help rid you of the frustration that occurs as the natural by-product of many employee interactions at work. Eat right, too, especially at lunch or when you're on the road. Develop a healthy routine and stick with it—no matter where you are.

- **Take a break.** When you take a break, you give your brain a much-needed chance to relax, and you allow yourself time to recharge your batteries. When you take a break, *really* take a break. Get away from the office for a while to avoid interruptions or, at the very least, close your door and turn off your phone.

- **Have fun.** About a third of our time is spent at work. If you're not having fun, why bother going? Sure, the money is important, but so is how you live your life while at work. Fun should be a central part of the relationships you share with others both at work and off the job.

- **Manage your schedule.** If you don't manage your own schedule, there's a good chance that someone else will be happy to manage it for you. Buy a quality personal planner or calendar and use it!

- **Be an optimist.** Don't automatically assume anything negative about anybody. Instead, look for the good in everyone you meet and in everything that you do. You'll be amazed at how much better your coworkers will feel about themselves when *you* are there to lift their spirits.

Overcoming Resistance

As anyone who has tried to change the status quo knows, dealing with organizational resistance can be a full-time job. According to Harvard professor and author John Kotter, organizational resistance can be defeated by applying the following steps:

1. Identify where all the relevant lateral relationships exist, including those that are subtle and almost invisible (in other words, figure out who needs to be led).

2. Assess who among these people may resist cooperation, why, and how strongly (figure out where the leadership challenge will be).

3. Develop, wherever possible, a good relationship with these people to facilitate the communication, education, or negotiation process required to reduce or overcome most kinds of resistance

(continued on next page)

without the planning or intervention of supervisors or managers. Says company president Lars Kolind, "I seldom tell anyone to do anything. People take action themselves." As a direct result of employees initiating action in a variety of ways, company profits have grown by a factor of six in only two years.

Looking for a way to help employees give something back to their community, Ed Benson, an employee at The Ken Blanchard Companies in Escondido, California, took the initiative to start a charity program on his own time. Benson and other employee volunteers met once a month during lunch to get the program off the ground. The charity now raises over $500,000 in donations from employees and their friends and families a year. And each year employees (who can also donate their time) get to vote on charities they'd most like to support. After seeing the success of this grassroots program, the company's management team allocated 10 percent of the company's pretax profits to be donated to community, educational, and religious organizations that have specific projects and programs devoted to such noble causes as decreasing the gap between the "haves" and the "have-nots," and helping those in temporary need.

Illinois Power Co. (IP) is a natural gas and electric utility based in Decatur, Illinois, that serves approximately 650,000 customers over a 15,000-square-mile area. A number of employees were concerned that the company's work procedures manual did not meet the needs of workers or the company. As a result, 5 full-time and 24 part-time employees pulled together to form a team to work on a project combining printed gas standards and maintenance documents into one user-friendly manual for its workers. Supervisors agreed to excuse individuals from their normal duties to work on the team, and after a few months, team members moved to special separate quarters to lessen unrelated interruptions.

According to Terry Firnkes, a service technician at IP, the result was a much more efficient and effective workforce. "It takes less time to look up information that you need to perform your job. We're getting the job done faster and more safely."

The new manual has also become a moneymaker for Illinois Power. IP prepared a brochure on the standards, sent it to other utilities, and subsequently sold the standards to City Public Service of San Antonio, New Orleans Public Service Inc., and Louisiana Gas Service Co. In addition, IP designed a standards logo for City Public Service, a gas/electric utility that employs about 2,000 people in San Antonio. City Public Service purchased the computerized version of the standards, and has signed a contract with IP to customize and revise the standards to the Texas utility's specifications for the next two years.

Enedelia Straughan, a project engineer for

(continued from previous page)

(develop the tools needed to lead).

4. And when Step 3 doesn't work by itself, carefully select and implement more subtle or more forceful methods to deal with the resistance (have the courage to lead).

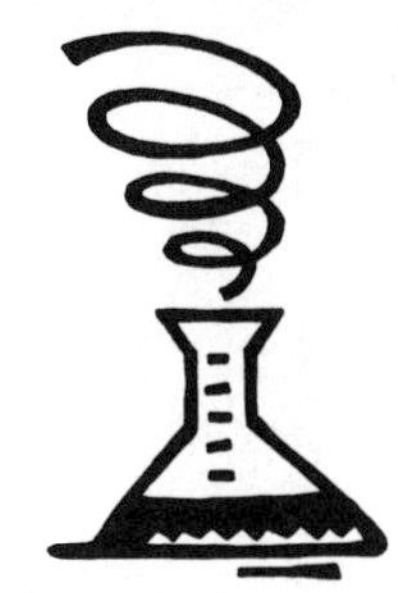

> "You've got to think about 'big things' while you're doing small things so that all the small things go in the right direction."
>
> —Alvin Toffler, Futurist and Writer

City Public Service, said her company bought IP's standards because "they were very detailed and ours weren't detailed enough. Their standards included a lot of procedures that our plan lacked. Most standards are not that detailed." Says team leader Don Johnson, "Marketing our standards to other utilities has enhanced our reputation within the industry. We want to create policies and procedures that set the best standard for our customers. It's part of striving to be the best."

A few years ago, Johnson & Johnson in New Brunswick, New Jersey, made the decision to market its famous baby oil for use as a suntan lotion. As the company prepared to launch its advertising campaign, some employees learned of the plan and voiced their objections, in part because the link between suntanning and skin cancer would be against the company's credo: "We believe our first responsibility is to the doctors, nurses, and patients, to mothers and all others who use our products and services." However, instead of simply being satisfied with successfully stopping the proposed marketing campaign, the employees took the initiative to suggest new alternative uses for the Johnson & Johnson baby oil. The result was a new campaign to use baby oil for removing makeup—an alternative that both met Johnson & Johnson's credo and provided the company with substantially increased revenues and profit.

When David Morris joined The Brady Group in Dallas, Texas, as a consultant several years ago, it didn't take him long to realize that the company could make improvements in the way it communicated with the outside world. The Brady Group helps call centers to write business plans, design telephone systems, and establish new call centers. Says Morris, "My job was to travel around the country doing analysis and design work for the company. After a few weeks, I noticed that there was a large void in the company when it came to marketing communications. The company was relying on its chairman and founder for all sales activity [cold calling]. I had previously done some web-page design with another company and had seen how significant a web presence can be: that company increased its good-quality leads by 25 percent using the web site. So, between travel assignments, I started designing web pages for The Brady Group, getting approval along the way as I developed the site, but not going through any lengthy advance approval or budgetary process." Now The Brady Group's web site is huge, well respected, and chock-full of information. The company has signed several large accounts that came to them via the web site.

> "Initiative is important in the workplace because it shows that you're ready to take on more responsibilities and make important decisions. If you do well it shows that you can learn, take on more responsibilities, and know how to advance your career."
>
> —Pauline, from the Internet

An engineer with one of the regional Bell phone companies formed by the breakup of AT&T became increasingly concerned about his organization's ability to keep up with its competitors. While the company trumpeted its

position on the leading edge of technology, its suppliers reported to the engineer that the company was actually far behind the pack. The engineer decided to do something about it. He first held an informal presentation with his work group over a brown-bag lunch to present his findings. He then wrote an internal memo comparing the company's technologies with those used by its competitors. After collecting more information, he scheduled a meeting with upper management to make his case. In response, the company launched a full-blown benchmarking effort of its core technologies. Not only did the company land on the leading edge of technology as a result, but it became dominant in the area of corporate business and was able to attract favorable deals with MCI and AT&T for long distance services.

It's one thing for a company to give its permission for employees to become more involved in the way they do their jobs, and another thing altogether for the newly liberated employees to put themselves to the test. When Pinnacle Brands, a manufacturer of sports trading cards in Grand Prairie, Texas, challenged its employees to manage themselves and to improve productivity in the process, undoubtedly some employees were wary about jumping into the fray. However, one secretary leapt at the opportunity. The woman, who was in charge of working with an outside firm that did trademark searches, determined that she could do the searches herself. By taking the initiative to

A Strategy

David Gee is program director for IBM's AlphaWorks "online laboratory" for Internet technology in San Jose, California. (AlphaWorks links Internet technology researchers with the Internet community, speeding the development of applications through the free and open exchange of ideas and technologies.) He offers the following advice for employees who want to make a difference at work:

1. You can't make a difference without doing things differently. Gee's mission is to pick up the pace of life at IBM. This means applying pressure to move faster. "My management tells me, 'If we're not getting four protest calls [from within IBM] a week, you're not doing your job.'"

2. People who sponsor change need sponsors. While Gee may exude self-confidence about his

(continued on next page)

suggest the idea and then put it into action, she saved Pinnacle $100,000 a year.

One day Vinny Petrillo, an assembler at United Electric Controls in Watertown, Massachusetts, asked a simple question: "Why do we have to do things this way?" Because the company was ordering a certain kind of switch that came with three unnecessary terminals, Petrillo spent as much as two hours a day removing those terminals. Petrillo's question prompted United Electric Controls to ask the same question of the vendor that supplied the switch. As it turned out, the supplier could provide a switch without the terminals; in fact, it would cost less. "I thought it was a good idea," Petrillo says proudly.

A few years ago, Ruth Inman, who is currently employed at Wittman-Hart, Inc., an information technology consulting firm in Peoria, Illinois, worked for Second Harvest–Chicago, a not-for-profit national food bank network. When Inman started with the company, Second Harvest had a six-month-old computer system that was effectively obsolete, because it had been purchased by an uninformed individual. The organization lacked the $6,000 necessary to upgrade the computer and make it useful again. Faced with a no-win situation, Inman decided to try a different approach. She called the computer company of her choice (Altos Computer Systems) and asked if it needed a tax

(continued from previous page)

status at IBM, he understands that he needs the help of company higher-ups to enable the AlphaWorks environment to grow and thrive. Gee spends a lot of time cultivating senior executives who will defend his approach and protect AlphaWorks from being hamstrung by questions from above: "We need air cover. We have people whose job it is to make sure complaints stick to *them* so we can continue our work."

3. Get results. Gee's team is gaining influence because of what it has achieved. "The first 90 days after we launched the [AlphaWorks web] site were critical," Gee says. "People came in droves. And they were people IBM was trying to reach, people who wouldn't have us on their radar screen if it weren't for AlphaWorks. We now have a proven track record."

write-off for that year. Would Altos be willing to donate a computer to her organization? Two weeks later the Altos system arrived, and it quickly became the main system, networking 25 to 30 employees who could then share data. Net savings? $6,000. Time saved by personnel not having to duplicate work? Exponential.

As Charles Chaser reviewed the computer inventory report at Cheeseborough-Ponds's distribution centers, he realized that stocks of Rose Awakening Cutex nail polish were down to a three-day supply—well below the three-and-a-half-week level that the company tries to keep on hand at all times. But Chaser was also aware that his own Jefferson City, Missouri, plant had shipped 346 dozen bottles of the polish just two days before. Rose Awakening must be "selling like hotcakes" he thought, and he knew something had to be done to prevent a major store shortage of the product. Chaser decided to take action. He turned to his terminal next to the production line and quickly typed in instructions to produce an extra 400 dozen bottles of the polish the very next morning. All a part of a scheduling manager's job, right? But Chaser isn't management. He's a line worker, one of hundreds who routinely tap the company's computer network to track shipments, schedule their own workloads, and perform the other functions that were once reserved only for management.

Making Goals Effective

Goals organized in a formal, systematic way are more likely to be achieved. Here are good ways to make your goals effective:

- Put your goals into writing.
- Link your work goals to the long-term vision of your organization.
- Link your personal goals to your long-term plans for career and life.
- Make sure your goals have measurable outcomes.
- Review progress toward your goals regularly, and adjust your goals as necessary to attain your overall objectives.
- Reward yourself whenever you attain a goal, or significant progress achieving it.

When the chairman of the board of Fort Worth, Texas–based electronics retailer Tandy Corporation (owner of the Radio Shack chain of stores) called 800-CEO-READ (formerly Schwartz Business Books of Milwaukee, Wisconsin) to find a book he had just heard about on cable channel CNBC, employee Roy Normington took the call. Although the Tandy chairman didn't know either the author or the title of the book, Normington went to work. He went to CNBC's web site and found a reference to the book, along with the author's name and the book's title. Normington immediately shipped the book to a very happy customer who proceeded to order copies for each of his managers.

> “Every company is looking for the person who will go the extra mile.”
>
> —DANGEROUSDAN, from the Internet

On one recent wintry morning in Toronto, Ontario, the weather was so bad that subway trains were halted, causing great consternation among the many commuters trying to get to their jobs downtown. At the Eglinton station, things were getting particularly dicey as the crowds grew and patrons began to get rowdy. Stuck along with the rest of the crowd was Chris Sanderson, an instructor at the Toronto Transit Commission's Surface Operations Training Centre. Seeing that the situation was quickly going from bad to worse, he decided to take action. Walking out of the station and across icy streets, Sanderson asked local coffee shops to donate coffee for the stuck transit patrons.

Although a couple of shops turned him

away, Sanderson persisted. Sure enough, Electric Beans, a cyber-café, came through, providing several jugs of hot coffee, cups, and workers to help pour it. While he couldn't make the trains start running, Sanderson was able to make his fellow riders a lot more comfortable while they waited.

TIPS FOR BEING IN CHARGE

1. Do not procrastinate. There's no time better than the present to do what needs to be done.

2. Constantly prioritize your work and do the most important things first. Priorities count! Save less important tasks for times when you have caught up with your most urgent issues.

3. Don't wait for others to make the first move. When something needs to be done, just get out there and do it!

4. Be a participant, not a spectator. You'll achieve your professional and personal goals much more quickly, and you'll be a happier, more productive person.

5. Take advantage of opportunities quickly. Many opportunities are fleeting: act on them before someone else does, or before the chance to act slips away!

Making Improvements

One of the easiest—and most effective—ways for employees to take initiative is to be on the lookout for ways to improve the work processes, products, services, and systems that are a vital part of how the organization does its business. No organization is perfect; there is always room for improvement and for new approaches to old problems. And if there is ever a place where *anyone* in an organization can take initiative, it's here. In fact, the person who does a job is in the best position to know how it can be done better. The lower you are in an organization's official hierarchy, the greater the chance that you have more contact with the *real* business—customers, clients, products, and services—than do those who are higher up the ladder. Clearly, *everyone* can make a significant contribution to his or her organization—one that will bring personal satisfaction, as well as a better bottom line for the company.

Author Tips

- Flesh out your ideas in a written proposal.
- Consider the costs and benefits of your ideas before you present them to management.
- Bounce your ideas off a colleague you trust.
- Seek informal support.
- Develop a plan for implementing your ideas.

Jerry Borchert, a power plant mechanic at Mary Kay, Inc., the cosmetics and personal-care products manufacturer based in Dallas, Texas, turned a dirty job into a bright idea—and saved the company more than $4,500 a month in the process.

Recently, a new waste-water treatment system was installed at the Mary Kay power plant. The new system helps keep the environment

A Better Way

- Imagine you were doing the task for the first time. Would you do it the way you are doing it now?
- If you had to, how could you do the task twice as fast? Five times as fast? Ten times as fast?
- Do you really need to do the task? What would happen if you skipped it?
- What would be a completely different way of doing the task?
- Can someone else do the task more easily?
- Look for ways to make new ideas work—not for reasons why they won't.
- Make a list of the things you would change in the company, if you could, along with your reasons for changing them. Prioritize the list and plan to take the top items to the next step.
- Learn informal ways of getting things done in your organization.

clean and reduces city waste-water cleaning charges. The system has proved successful, removing at least 99 percent of oil, wax, and grease left from cleaning the kettles and tanks, which are used to manufacture the company's products. However, the waste separator, the workhorse of the system, removed about ten times more oil than anticipated.

To keep up with the separator's production, Jerry, a power plant mechanic, spent three to four hours a day manually pumping the oil into 55-gallon drums—a dirty, exhausting, and costly job. He knew that there had to be a better way. So he set out to design an automatic pumping system. "I prayed to God for guidance," says Borchert, "and I got the inspiration to build a network of pipes that would drop down to the water's surface, hook up to a pump, and drain the oil into a 2,000-gallon tank."

Borchert sketched his idea on paper and presented it to power plant supervisor Walt Bechtol. It took Borchert only a few days and less than $200 in materials to put the system to work. Thanks to Borchert's initiative, it's now a fairly easy job to clean the waste separator. It takes only 30 to 45 minutes per shift instead of three to four hours. Also, pumping the oil into a 2,000-gallon tank instead of 55-gallon drums saves the company money. A larger tank reduces the number of times the tank is emptied by the disposal company, dropping disposal costs from $1.75 a gallon to 25 cents a gallon, saving Mary Kay $50,000 to $60,000 per year.

HOW TO MAKE SUGGESTIONS COUNT

BE YOUR OWN BOSS

An important aspect of initiative that any employee can put into practice is making suggestions. Every employer wants and needs employees who can spot problem areas and suggest improvements in a sincere, constructive manner. Here are some tips on how to maximize your effectiveness in making suggestions where you work:

Start in your own area. You can best impact the area you know the most about. In your current job, look for ways to save money, improve service, or streamline processes. Experiment as necessary to test your ideas.

Have a plan for implementation. Suggestions can sound like complaints if there is no plan for their implementation. Think through the costs and benefits of your idea and how you can make—or initiate—the desired change. Document your suggestion and share it with others. Consider who else would need to be involved to implement the suggestion and seek the input, involvement, and approval of those individuals as soon as possible. Own your ideas: to see them to fruition, volunteer to do those aspects of the suggestion that you're able to implement. Learn how to sell your ideas to others.

Develop a mind-set for making suggestions. Think about potential improvements during transition times, such as when you commute to work. Try to develop a minimum of two ideas a week that you can submit or share with others for making improvements. Carry a notepad and pen or pencil with you to jot down ideas.

Support and build on other people's suggestions. By supporting other people's ideas, you'll develop good will and alliances that can be beneficial when you need help and support.

Don't Settle for Just Good Enough

1. Look for ways to make improvements to the status quo, and follow through with a plan of action.
2. Focus your suggestions on areas that have the greatest impact on the organization.
3. Follow up your suggestions with action. Volunteer to help implement your suggestions.
4. Step outside of your box. Look for areas of improvement throughout your organization, not just within your own department or business unit.
5. Don't make frivolous suggestions. They degrade your credibility and distract you from more important areas of improvement.

While working for Berkeley Challenge, a cleaning company in Brisbane, Australia, crew leader Alison Philippe had long wondered how to make the process of cleaning the Brisbane Entertainment Centre, a large sports and entertainment facility, more efficient and cost-effective. Her lead employee, Peter Thistlethwaite, asked if he could try organizing a better way to get the job done. A week after Philippe said yes, Thistlethwaite came back with an organized method of cleaning the seating area that decreased the labor cost by almost 15 percent. Not only that, but the quality of the work improved and the staff's motivation increased as employees actively sought to give their own input about how to improve the cleaning process. Says Philippe, "I was so impressed by the change that I eventually left the company and returned to school to learn how to manage people properly and effectively."

Concerned that many potential customers with regular day jobs were unable to shop during the majority of time that his store was open, an employee at one of Kacey's Fine Furniture's retail stores in Denver, Colorado, decided to figure out a way to fix this problem. His idea was simple: change the store's operating hours to times that were more convenient for working customers. The idea was adopted by management and resulted in a 15 percent increase in sales.

Employees at electronics manufacturing giant Motorola have learned that taking initiative on the job can result in substantial gains for both the company and them. When Motorola's cable modem manufacturing plant in Mansfield, Massachusetts, had only six weeks to document the production steps required for assembly of a new unit—a process that usually took months—Blane McMichen, manager of production technologies, decided to use an organization-wide intranet rather than paper. McMichen asked for employee feedback on the new system, and many of the suggestions, such as putting more specifications on each screen and reducing the time spent clicking between sections, dramatically increased the efficiency of workers using the system, saving the company both time and money. Motorola rolled out the new paperless assembly system at its Huntsville, Alabama, and Schaumburg, Illinois, plants.

> “Initiative is the key to any business. If you have the guts to stick with your ideas and be able to pick yourself up after you have fallen, you will make it in this world. You can't succeed if you don't make mistakes and go on. If you have confidence in yourself then you will have the initiative to go forward.”
>
> —WFT, from the Internet

The Arbitron Company in Columbia, Maryland, is a leader in information services. The company's primary business is rating radio programs and doing qualitative demographic research. Arbitron's interviewers call respondents and ask them to fill out a survey (or seven-day diary) tracking their radio listening for a seven-day period. This information is used by advertisers and ad agencies in selling advertising time on radio stations. The Survey Mailing Department mails diaries to respondents. Diaries are mailed in envelopes, or for some key sample

> “The person who displays initiative is always looking for a more efficient way of working, which is a positive benefit to any organization.”
>
> —MARCIA, from the Internet

households, in boxes about the size of the container that people receive their checkbooks in. In 1995, Arbitron was mailing about 30,000 of these boxes each year.

During the spring survey of 1995, Dave Tennent was working on the job of sealing the survey boxes prior to mailing them. This last step in the process was quite labor-intensive and therefore very expensive and slow. The boxes had a paper flap that needed to be sealed, and the employees sealed the boxes by hand, using a wet sponge. Tennent knew that the number of boxes to be mailed was going to increase, and that this could pose a potential bottleneck, so he set out to find a way to improve this process.

He went to a local business that made shrinkwrap and had a few of the boxes wrapped with it. Then he took a sample to his team with a proposal explaining his idea. The equipment cost the company about $13,000, but it would eventually save more than $15,000 a year in labor. It also resulted in a better-quality product. The idea was approved within a few weeks. The following year Tennent showed initiative in other quality improvements and went on to be recognized as an “AllStar” through Arbitron's All-Stars Program, a formal recognition program in which employees are nominated by their peers. The award is a company-sponsored trip for All-Stars winners, their guests, and company executives.

Ruth Inman's job at Wittman-Hart, Inc., an information technology consulting firm in Peoria, Illinois, is to teach people from other companies how to use Lotus Notes software. One of the weekly e-mails that circulates around her office is from the company's recruiters announcing new positions that are open that week. Because employees get bonuses for any leads or referrals they submit, the e-mail contains two file attachments with the referral forms that employees need to print out, manually fill out, and hand to the recruiters.

Since Wittman-Hart is an information technology firm, Inman wondered why this process wasn't handled electronically. She mentioned to the company's recruiters that the task could be accomplished electronically, and they would not have to keep sending file attachments in their e-mail (which also used up precious hard drive space on the company's servers). But while the recruiters loved the idea, they didn't have time to implement her suggestion. Inman volunteered to develop a database to hold the referral forms. Now, when the weekly e-mail goes out to employees, it has a "pointer" readers can click on that "jumps" them to the form. They simply fill out the form on their computer, click, and send. Says Inman, "I believe that if people just stuck to doing 'their own job' some things would never get done!"

> "There's no one grand stroke that does it. It's a lot of little steps."
>
> —PETER A. COHEN, Chairman, Shearson Lehman Brothers

In a quality-improvement initiative spearheaded by employees working for the city of New York Department of Parks and Recreation,

staff independently figured out a way to increase the number of diseased, damaged, or destructive trees removed by each work crew from four or five per day to ten or eleven per day, at the same time the number of people on each crew was reduced from seven to four. The result was a savings of $114,000 for each crew.

> “Nothing in the world can take the place of persistence.”
>
> —Calvin Coolidge

SELLING YOUR IDEAS TO OTHERS

Often, taking initiative requires that you convince others to support your point of view. Here are tips on presenting your ideas to others:

■ **Outline your goals.** What are you trying to accomplish? Do you want to convince your boss to try a new approach to solve a customer-service problem? Perhaps you'd like to form a committee to develop ways to improve the environmental friendliness of your firm? First outline your goals in writing, and then hone them before you present them to your target audience.

■ **Develop a list of the positive points of your plan.** Decide on the key advantages of using your ideas and collect data—both qualitative and quantitative—that support your plan. These few major points will form the backbone of your presentation.

■ **Do a negative-objection analysis.** Think through the questions and objections your proposal is likely to receive. Develop a sound response for each and collect the additional data and evidence you need to make your case.

■ **Presell your plan.** Informally approach others whose opinion you respect to get their feedback on your proposal. Not only will you find ways to improve your plan, but those who are involved in the review process will begin to buy into your proposal.

Beverly Scibilia of United Electric Controls in Watertown, Massachusetts, had the complex and strenuous job of assembling temperature controls for large hospital sterilizers. Knowing there must be a way to reduce the amount of time and effort required to complete the process, she pulled together a group of coworkers to watch her use the large, heavy press and then offer ideas on how to improve the process. Scibilia took their suggestions and worked with the model shop to design a new machine. What used to take an hour now takes no more than 15 minutes. Another machine, which works on the same principle, reduced setup time from 45 minutes to a matter of seconds. According to Scibilia, the time it takes for her to get out an order now is just a fraction of what it was before: "What took me six weeks before, I can now get out in a week."

> "Although intelligence is very important as part of the work ethic, initiative takes a much more important role in workplaces. It is very easy for employers and employees to think of good ideas, but it is often difficult to have someone take responsibility for those ideas. It's pointless to have good ideas 'just sitting around.' Someone has to act on them."
>
> —STEFAN NAM, from the Internet

Innovative employees at the Conoco oil refinery in Ponca City, Oklahoma, which produces motor fuels, lubricants, and specialty products from petroleum, developed and implemented improvements that resulted in a 5,000-barrel-per-day increase in the oil output of the No. 2 crude oil treatment unit.

Suspecting that there might be ways to improve performance at New York City's Sanitation Department, a group of motor-equipment operators within the department took the initiative to interview their 1,200 coworkers to get

> "Even if you are intelligent, have good ideas, and know everything, without initiative you're just waiting for orders from your boss. You can guess the result."
>
> —Chi Jingxing, from the Internet

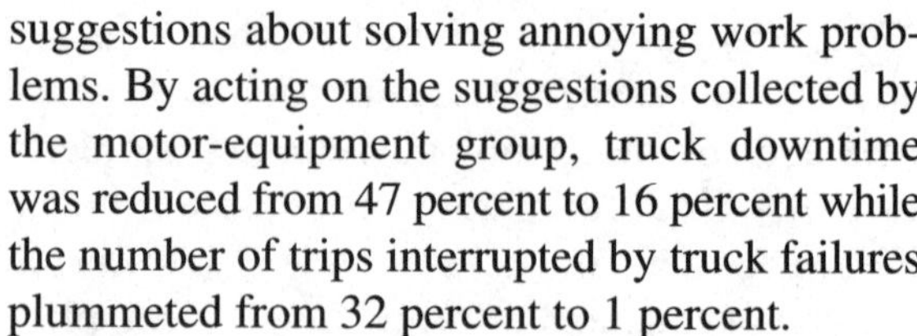

suggestions about solving annoying work problems. By acting on the suggestions collected by the motor-equipment group, truck downtime was reduced from 47 percent to 16 percent while the number of trips interrupted by truck failures plummeted from 32 percent to 1 percent.

Spurred on by the challenge of finding ways to reduce manufacturing costs and improve worker effectiveness, employees at 3M's manufacturing plant in Cumberland, Wisconsin, independently identified and implemented cost reductions that reduced unit manufacturing costs for Scotch-Brite Floor Pads by 30 percent and virtually eliminated waste.

When phone-information employees at Washington's Department of Metropolitan Services (King County) took the initiative to go outside their offices to learn how their customers actually experienced the services that they delivered, they were able to make numerous improvements to the call-handling system. As a result, calls handled increased dramatically from 50 percent to 90 percent, the average customer wait time plunged from 157 seconds to 65 seconds, and accuracy increased.

At Syncrude Canada, Ltd., headquartered in Fort McMurray, Alberta, Canada, employees have long been concerned about how to cut back on waste and improve the environment,

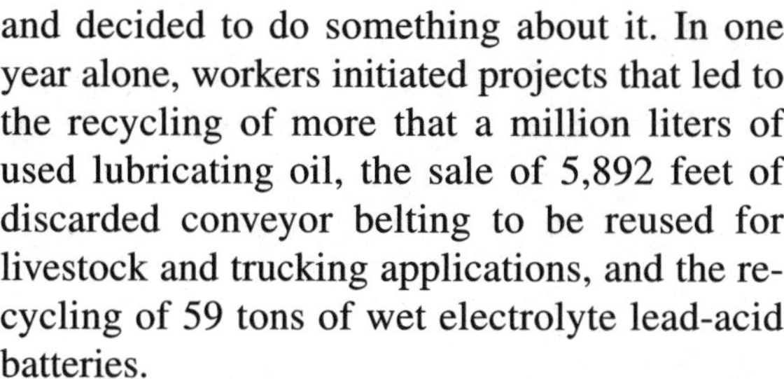

and decided to do something about it. In one year alone, workers initiated projects that led to the recycling of more that a million liters of used lubricating oil, the sale of 5,892 feet of discarded conveyor belting to be reused for livestock and trucking applications, and the recycling of 59 tons of wet electrolyte lead-acid batteries.

> “Intelligence without initiative is a smart person who doesn't want to work. Inspiration without initiative is a person with great ideas but no resolve to follow through. Without initiative work would not get done.”
>
> —CHRIS VAN GEEST, from the Internet

At Beth Israel Medical Center in Boston, Massachusetts, employees decided they could save more than $200 per blood transfusion by collecting their own blood. They established a donor area, where employees make regular blood donations.

Complaints received about the long delay between the time employees requested the purchase of materials and the time they were received led workers from the Information Services and Finance and Procurement Groups at aerospace manufacturer Lockheed Martin Missiles and Space Company in Sunnyvale, California, to initiate a new procedure. They designed artificial intelligence software to be added to the company's Fastbuy software. The new software, dubbed ASAP (Advisory System for Automated Procurement), scans the Fastbuy database looking for common errors and either resolves them automatically or gives a pop-up message to the user, who can then make changes on-screen before forwarding the document to Procurement. William Shirado and

> “Initiative is #1. A certain amount of intelligence is certainly needed to get the job and keep the job. ‘New ideas’ are not welcome in all jobs, but when they are and you’ve come up with an unusual and productive one, that could be the key that unlocks future upward mobility.”
>
> —WILLIAM HUBBELL, JR., from the Internet

Robin Pape coordinated the design of the new system, interviewing users at every step of the way. The new system handled 25,000 requests from 1,000 people and saved $1.8 million in the first year, Shirado estimates.

After a coworker was burned when the equipment he was working on malfunctioned, a group of employees at the University of Delaware in Newark were concerned that workers injured on the job might lose precious moments waiting for local firefighters and rescue teams to arrive. To solve this potentially disastrous problem, the employees formed the First Aid Service Team (FAST), composed of employees who are active emergency medical technicians and rescue personnel outside of working hours. Instead of interfering with this employee initiative or dampening the spirits of those who participated, management actively supported the effort. Says Ron Beaver, an electronics technician and FAST member, “I think it was pretty nice of management to work with us. They were open with us and provided the equipment.” In praising the team, Thomas Vacha, assistant vice president of facilities, noted, “It was an employee initiative. They provided the justification and gave us a list of the needed materials.”

When a staffer at Dana Corporation got wind of the company’s plan to build additional parking lots at its plant in Elizabethtown,

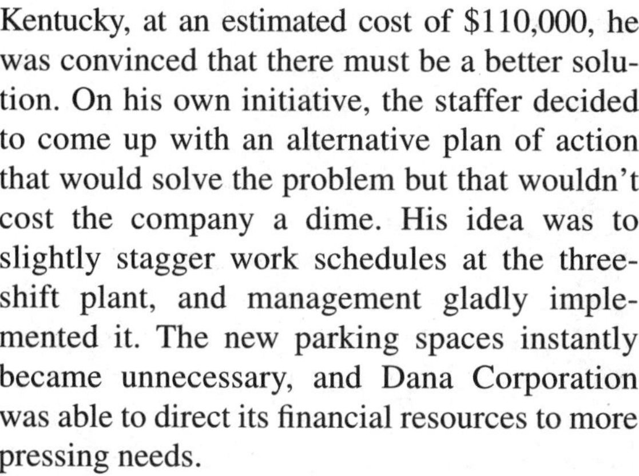

Kentucky, at an estimated cost of $110,000, he was convinced that there must be a better solution. On his own initiative, the staffer decided to come up with an alternative plan of action that would solve the problem but that wouldn't cost the company a dime. His idea was to slightly stagger work schedules at the three-shift plant, and management gladly implemented it. The new parking spaces instantly became unnecessary, and Dana Corporation was able to direct its financial resources to more pressing needs.

> "If you put off everything till you're sure of it, you'll get nothing done."
>
> —NORMAN VINCENT PEALE, *The Power of Positive Thinking*

At Cerdec Corporation, a manufacturer of pigments and colorants for the international glass, ceramics, and plastics industries located in Washington, Pennsylvania, a lab employee had a great idea. Whenever a worker's suggestion is implemented, a bright metallic sticker is placed near the location of the machine, office, or area affected by the suggestion. The implementation date and name of the employee who made the suggestion is noted along with the caption "UNITE SUCCESS STORY, Thumbs Up for That Great Idea" (UNITE is the name of Cerdec's Scanlon Plan process for encouraging employee involvement). Workers at Cerdec are as proud to receive and show off their UNITE suggestion stickers as the company is to receive and implement their suggestions. To date, employees have submitted more than 3,000 suggestions and more than 2,000 have been implemented. Total savings to the company has amounted to more than $6.5 million;

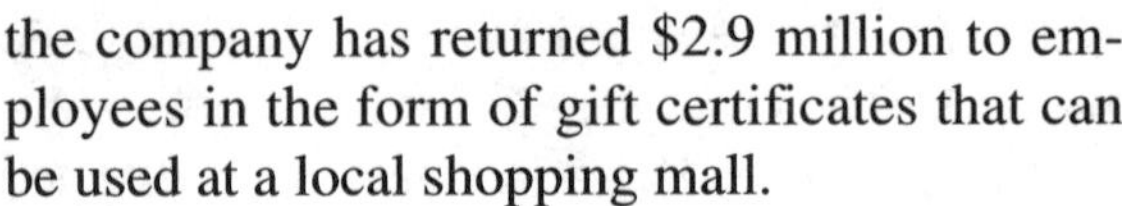

the company has returned $2.9 million to employees in the form of gift certificates that can be used at a local shopping mall.

Companies around the world have discovered that making the move to ecologically sound practices, such as recycling and reducing waste generated in manufacturing and administrative processes, is not only good for the earth, but also can have a positive influence on the bottom line. To help meet Northern Telecom's paper purchase reduction targets, employees of their internal distribution department in St. John, New Brunswick, Canada, hit upon the idea of charging other departments in the organization an average of $1,000 for each request for printed documentation. Departments requesting documentation on CD-ROM would pay only about $23. This initiative has resulted in huge reductions in paper consumption.

> “There are a couple of routes you can take [to get a new idea approved by management]. You can go to the top first and try to convince them to direct the change, or you can go to parallel levels and get their buy-in so that you can go to management together with a new idea. I'm a big advocate of the latter.”
>
> —JOE ANDRASKI, Group Vice President, Integrated Logistics, Nabisco Foods

---

An axle welder in the massive John Deere & Company tractor manufacturing factory in Moline, Illinois, was getting annoyed. In order to obtain a needed spare part or to get an update on a particular item, he would have to walk all over the factory, wasting both his and his colleagues' time. So, what did he do? He did what any other progressive-thinking axle welder would do; he presented the problem and a suggested solution to his boss! After hearing the welder's presentation, the boss quickly approved purchase of a cellular phone for his worker. The increased

productivity of the worker has more than paid for the original investment.

Jacie Rubenstein, an employee at the company headquarters of Mervyn's department store in Hayward, California, undertook a temporary assignment in the company's boys' department. While attending the merchandise team's weekly meetings, Rubenstein noticed that they didn't include a detailed review of that week's advertising schedules, a review that was an important part of the meeting agenda for many of Mervyn's other divisions. Knowing that adding this review to the boys' department's meetings would be an effective way to improve performance, she suggested that the department do just that. Rubenstein's suggestion was accepted, and the advertising schedule review became a regular part of the meeting agenda.

> "You need initiative to get ahead anywhere. Show you can and will do whatever is necessary to get the job done."
>
> —PAUL, from the Internet

Employees who put their heads together to seek solutions can often surprise their colleagues with the good things that result. Such was the case with Linda Reed and Vicki Edwards, two quality-control employees at GGS Information Services, an information technology firm in York, Pennsylvania. After five years of hard service to the company, two Hewlett-Packard laser printers in dire need of repair were determined to be unsalvageable by the manufacturer's technicians. Undaunted, Reed and Edwards asked Paul Kilker, CEO of GGS Information Services, if they could try to bring

Innovation Is Unpredictable

Many if not most innovations come from the "wrong" places: mavericks with an obsession about something, individuals stumbling across new discoveries by accident, people finding new uses for products intended for different markets, and so on. After 25 years of studying IBM, General Electric, Polaroid, and Xerox, Brian Quinn of the Amos Tuck Business School of Dartmouth College found that not a single product had come from a formal planning process.

the units back to life. With nothing to lose, Kilker agreed. The pair fashioned a crude repair tool by duct-taping a few straws to the hose of a small vacuum cleaner. Reed and Edwards then used their homemade cleaning device to remove years' worth of toner and dust buildup. Sure enough, the idea worked, and the printers went on to produce millions more pages. Reed and Edwards's invention has been used on all office printers not already covered by a service contract. Says Kilker about the pair, "They're pretty ingenious. We saved the cost of at least two new printers."

Perseverance and Persistence

If there are heroes among those employees who choose to take initiative on the job, their stories are usually ones of extraordinary perseverance and persistence against higher-ups or entrenched policies and systems that work to ensure the maintenance of the status quo. It often takes a fair amount of guts to take initiative in the first place. But to persist—even when you seem defeated or, worse, you've been directed to no longer do so—takes an incredible amount of fortitude. During the course of developing the light bulb, inventor Thomas Edison tried a thousand different materials for the bulb's filament. All failed. When asked if he felt that all this time was wasted, Edison replied, "Hardly. I have discovered a thousand things that don't work." As the following examples show, the rewards for persistence can be great, both for the individual and for the organization.

Never, Never, Never Give Up

- Ninety percent of the value occurs in the last one percent of effort.
- Be good at those things others dislike.
- Always do your best.
- The status quo is a very powerful force in any organization. Question authority. Be polite but determined.

Soon after Yumi started in an entry-level position at a Hitachi silicon-wafer fabrication plant in Japan, she learned that management was reviewing a proposal to close the plant due to a defect rate some 20 percent higher than the norm. Riding to work one day on her bike, Yumi noticed that a passing train caused her handlebars to vibrate. Armed with this discovery, she suggested to the plant manager that perhaps there was a link between the high

> “Success depends on people. It’s not difficult for intelligent people to come up with creative ideas. The key is to follow through. Surround yourself with talented, competent people who share your goals and believe in the program.”
>
> —Dale Browning, President, Plus System, Inc.

defect rate and passing trains. Although skeptical about Yumi’s theory, he passed her idea on to Hitachi’s corporate quality engineers, who conducted vibration tests, but came up empty-handed. Yumi didn’t lose faith in her idea. She did more research and discovered that some low-frequency vibrations could escape detection, but still have a negative effect. Yumi convinced management to try building a moat filled with water between the train tracks and the plant. A group of employee volunteers took on the project one weekend. To almost everyone’s surprise, the idea worked and the plant was saved from the wrecking ball.

The design team for a new locomotive at General Electric’s Transportation Systems Division manufacturing plant in Erie, Pennsylvania, was explicitly told four times by management to “cease and desist” in their efforts to develop a new type of locomotive. However, because of their energy and commitment, the members of the team ignored management’s demands, continued their work, and succeeded in developing a locomotive that now accounts for a significant portion of the company’s total business.

Management at Disneyland in Anaheim, California, rarely brings retired rides back to life. It’s therefore no surprise that most requests to do so, whether from park visitors or employees, are flatly turned down. However,

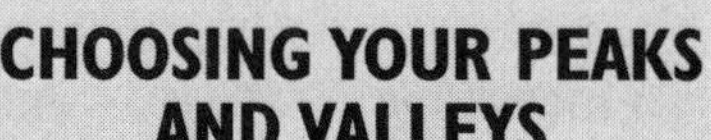

CHOOSING YOUR PEAKS AND VALLEYS

While it's true that persistence is a desirable trait, you also need to learn when to back down at work. Taking initiative takes energy. Thus you need to learn to use your energy on those issues that are most important to you—and ones you can achieve given your existing resources. The following questions will help you to determine your priorities and decide if the time is right to pursue your goal.

How important is the goal to you? You first need to be clear about your own motivation. Why do you think your goal will benefit the organization? What evidence do you have that achieving the goal will help? Does the goal align with your personal values and objectives? What will you personally gain from achieving the goal? Is it in sync with your boss's priorities and values? With the organization's mission and values?

What allies and opponents do you have for achieving the goal? In any organization, support from others is a critical component for achieving most goals. Does your manager support your goal? Do others in the organization feel your objective is worthwhile? Could you make use of any favors to gain support for your goal? Is anyone in higher management strongly for or strongly against your goal?

Do the odds favor achieving your goal? What plan do you have for achieving the goal? Has a similar plan worked in the organization? If your idea makes sense, why hasn't it been done before? Is the effort worth the risk of failure? What are the costs versus the benefits of the goal?

An upfront analysis of any desired objective can help you determine if your goal is realistic to pursue given the current circumstances in your organization.

> “Our people . . . are responsible for their own product and its quality. We expect them to act like owners.”
>
> —Gordon Forward, President, Chaparral Steel

when a small but persistent group of workers recently pushed for the return of the dry-docked Huck Finn keelboats and their wisecracking river pilots, the powers-that-be agreed to do just that. Not only was the ride taken out of mothballs, but management put the workers who took the initiative to bring Huck Finn back to life in charge of the revived ride.

Hewlett-Packard engineer Charles House was given a medal for “extraordinary contempt and defiance beyond the normal call of engineering duty.” Why? He had ignored an order from company founder David Packard to stop working on a type of high-quality video monitor. Despite the rebuke, House pressed ahead and succeeded in developing the monitor, which was used to track NASA’s manned moon landings and is also used in heart transplants. Although early estimates indicated that the market for such large-screen displays would be only 30 units, more than 17,000 of them—worth about $35 million—were sold.

Lorin Industries, a manufacturer of anodized aluminum products located in Muskegon, Michigan, believes in the Scanlon philosophy (see page 6) of participative management. Jim Nalewick, a project chemist working in Lorin’s technical lab, had an idea that involved changing the company’s waste-treatment process by replacing sodium hydroxide with lime neutralization. Although it took a year and a half for

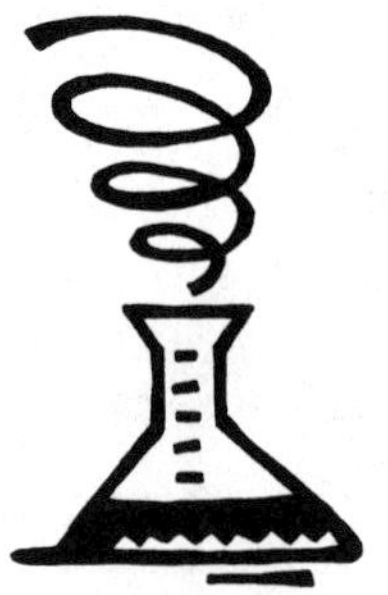

management to approve his idea because of the high cost of the proposed process conversion, Nalewick stuck to his guns, and the plan was ultimately approved and implemented. The result? An annual savings of $500,000. And Lorin Industries received the Muskegon Area Environmental Excellence Award.

> “The sequence to success is to reimagine the world, reengineer the process, and then use information systems to glue it all together. Sometimes new ideas can be a little cloudy. You have to believe that things can be done, even if you don't know exactly how it will work.”
>
> —DENNIS COLARD, Corporate Logistics Manager, Hewlett-Packard Corporation

---

In the late 1970s, well before personal computers became a household staple, John Roach, then the vice president of manufacturing at Tandy Corporation in Fort Worth, Texas, and now CEO, became convinced that selling personal computers through the company's Radio Shack electronics stores could be a real moneymaker. However, when he pitched the idea to his bosses, they declined, believing that personal computers were still the stuff of dreamers. Rebuffed, but not disheartened, Roach pulled together a team of coworkers to build a working prototype of the computer he had in mind. Armed with his prototype, he again pitched his idea to management—this time successfully. Radio Shack went on to become a major player in the early history of personal computers.

Emily Rodriguez, corporate director of transportation for Esprit de Corp, a San Francisco–based clothing manufacturer, was convinced that consolidating overseas product orders into fewer but larger shipments was necessary for Esprit to control its imports. When she first submitted a proposal to the vice

MANAGING YOUR TIME

Taking initiative can often mean taking charge of your own time. Time management is not something you can do once and then just forget. It takes ongoing effort and commitment to ensure that you're always acting on the things that are most important and not distracted by the many trivial things that vie for your attention. If you follow these tips, you'll be sure to use your time wisely more often than not:

1. At the end of each workday, before you go home, make a to-do list for the next day; prioritize by placing your most important tasks at the top and your least important tasks at the bottom.

2. Arrive at your office at least a half hour early and reserve this "quiet" time to work uninterrupted on your highest-priority task.

3. Don't work on lower-priority tasks before you are completely satisfied with the progress you have made on your higher-priority tasks.

4. Buy and use a day-planning calendar or system.

5. Go through your in-box at least once a day and prioritize the contents. Deal with routine correspondence promptly instead of allowing it to pile up.

6. Opt out of unimportant meetings, and attend those that can help you achieve your goals and objectives.

7. Focus on doing the work that you are uniquely qualified to do. Delegate the rest to your coworkers.

8. Set aside a couple of uninterrupted hours every week to think about the "big picture" and your long-term goals and objectives, and to develop strategies for attaining them.

9. Learn how to say no, politely but firmly.

president of operations, it was deep-sixed. Undaunted, she maintained up-to-date information supporting her contention. One year later, when it was apparent to upper management that something had to be done, she was able to immediately provide fresh information to augment the year-old proposal. She was on the next plane to Asia with orders to set up the program.

> "There is no security on this earth; there is only opportunity."
>
> —DOUGLAS MACARTHUR, Former Five-Star General of the U.S. Army

---

Bill McLain, in his sixties and jobless after 40 years as a technical writer and publications manager, reluctantly took a position at Xerox in Palo Alto, California, answering e-mail sent to Xerox's web site. He soon found that in the midst of queries about printers and digital imaging he received a number of rather unusual inquiries, such as "What are the words to *Kumbaya*?" His boss told him not to bother, but McLain looked up the lyrics anyway and replied. Now, McLain routinely fields such questions as "Where did the idea for underwear come from?" and "Who's the richest man in the world?" He's also asked for dating advice. The address—webmaster@xerox.com—gets about 350 questions a day. Xerox has assigned three assistants to McLain to handle the workload, which has resulted in a significant increase in highly desirable traffic on the corporation web site.

A self-managing team of employees at a small manufacturer of plastic injection molded parts kept getting calls from the company's finishing department regarding an ongoing

“It is not sufficient for people to do their assigned jobs.”

—AL PIETRASANTA, Program Manager, IBM

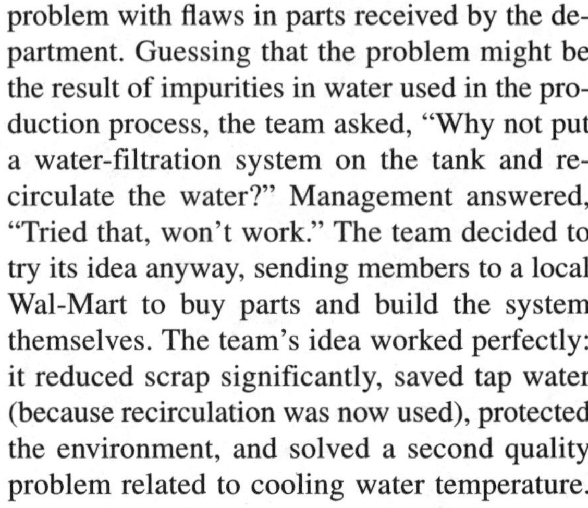

problem with flaws in parts received by the department. Guessing that the problem might be the result of impurities in water used in the production process, the team asked, “Why not put a water-filtration system on the tank and recirculate the water?” Management answered, “Tried that, won’t work.” The team decided to try its idea anyway, sending members to a local Wal-Mart to buy parts and build the system themselves. The team’s idea worked perfectly: it reduced scrap significantly, saved tap water (because recirculation was now used), protected the environment, and solved a second quality problem related to cooling water temperature.

Bob Comeau of United Electric Controls in Watertown, Massachusetts, wanted to relieve the pain he endured when carrying spools of wire, which can weigh as much as 50 pounds apiece, around his work area. “Lifting those things was painful and time consuming,” he says. Comeau often imagined what it would be like to have a rack with wheels that would hold 35 or so of the giant rolls so he could move them to the cutting, measuring, and stripping machine. He decided to take action by experimenting with a version that would hold just six rolls, but that proved dangerous. “The thing could tip easily,” he says. However, Comeau remained committed to the concept. “I knew this could really save time,” he says. After many unsuccessful attempts, he finally hit upon the answer: build immobile racks for the spools and mount the machine on wheels. Now Comeau

simply wheels the machine, pushing it like a supermarket cart, to the appropriate spool of wire. As a result, today the wire-assembly department is more productive with two people than it used to be with seven.

As customer-service manager for GE Medical Systems in Milwaukee, Wisconsin, Tom Owens had tried for years to get his organization to adopt a new recruiting program. Eventually, his boss agreed and Owens funded the project with internal-department funds—all the while trying to secure the corporate funds necessary to expand and fully implement the program. After two years of trying to convince others of the merit of the new recruiting program, a new general manager agreed and obtained the several hundred thousand dollars Owens needed to make his dream a reality.

Josiah, a housing-mortgage specialist at a Fortune 500 bank, knew that he was most productive from about 10:00 A.M. until the early evening hours. However, his employer insisted that all employees show up at 7:00 A.M. Eventually, a new CEO came on board, and Josiah took the opportunity to propose a flex-time program. The CEO agreed, and soon many of the department's workers shifted their schedules to a 10:00 A.M. start time. Productivity soared among the workers who moved to the new flex-time schedule. Both Josiah and his company

> “Initiative uses intelligence, critical thinking, expertise, and other motivating factors to improve performance and productivity. It enables the individual to take on challenging tasks with confidence and to work toward organizational goals.”
>
> —Chris Sunguti, from the Internet

benefited from his concerted effort to push his good idea up the organizational ladder.

> “Organization can never be a substitute for initiative and for judgment.”
>
> —Louis Dembitz Brandeis, U.S. Supreme Court Justice

After trying out several ideas for new products on Bell Atlantic's internal entrepreneurship review board in New York City, only to be sent away empty-handed each time, employee Jack Copley finally hit the target with a graphics software program called Thinx. After testing the idea and developing a business plan, Copley became head of a 20-member team that developed the software, worked out glitches, chose the name, and designed packaging. Thinx hit the market to rave reviews, and Copley was named one of five finalists for a *Discover* magazine award honoring engineers and scientists who make technological breakthroughs.

PERSISTENCE PAYS OFF

TAKE ACTION NOW!

1. Focus on what you *can* do, not on what you *can't* do. Put your energy to good use working toward your goals instead of working against them.

2. Don't give up. Your next victory might be just over the horizon.

3. Look for ways to get others to say yes. No one likes to tell an associate no—give others lots of options and reasons to say yes, instead.

4. Identify roadblocks to your goals and then dismantle them one by one. The more roadblocks you remove, the quicker you'll reach your goals.

5. Be assertive, not aggressive. Be polite, but persistent.

PART II

YOU AND OTHERS

Every organization is a social community and, as a result, employees have to be skilled at working with others to get things done. The ability to do this effectively is a critical skill in business, and it can mean the difference between success and failure; therefore, employees need to take initiative to maximize their professional relationships.

By leading others, selling an idea, managing up, working in teams, or serving the customer beyond their expectations, the best employees know how to get things done with others in their organization. Savvy employees who ask for assistance or advice can obtain results that they couldn't achieve on their own.

Working with others, especially in teams, can make taking initiative an easier prospect. Having the support of coworkers, as well as the benefit of their unique experience and expertise, is a sure way of multiplying the effectiveness of

your own efforts. Not only that, but the very nature of teams themselves—with team members constantly seeking new and better ways of getting things done and responding to customer needs and desires—can go a long way toward generating the momentum needed for initiative to flourish in an organization.

Employees today cannot afford to sit back and wait for their managers, coworkers, or customers to come to them with ideas and solutions—they must be on the lookout for opportunities to be proactive, to anticipate the needs of others, and to meet those needs. Those who do will have a positive and lasting impact not just on their careers but on their coworkers, customers, and organizations, too.

Leadership and Influence

Self-leadership is the essence of initiative; it's putting yourself in charge of your work without constant intervention and monitoring by your manager. It's making decisions yourself instead of waiting for your manager to make decisions for you. And what happens when employees manage themselves? In a recent survey of senior managers, direct employee involvement in decision making, including taking initiative, was cited as the major factor in increased productivity in the last five years.

Leadership knows no boundaries, and leaders can be found anywhere in a company, regardless of an employee's place on the organizational chart. In a recent study entitled *Liberating Leadership Report,* published by the United Kingdom's Industrial Society, more than 80 percent of those identified by employees as having genuine leadership ability are not in positions of formal authority. Another study showed that, on average, the formal leaders of an organization contribute no more than 20 percent to the success of most organizations; followers are critical to the remaining 80 percent.

While managers use policies, procedures, milestones, and the like to *push* their associates to achieve the goals of the organization, leaders *inspire* their associates to achieve the goals of the organization through their actions and their example. All it takes to be a leader is a vision of the way things should be, the passion to convince others to join you, and the initiative to get the ball rolling. As Ken Blanchard, management guru and coauthor of *The One-Minute Manager,* says, "The key to successful leadership today is influence, not authority."

Anyone Can Be a Leader

- Influence = Power.
- People are persuaded differently. Find the hot buttons and push them.
- Enlist the support of others and ask them to join you in your efforts to improve your organization.
- Act in the best interests of the group.
- Express the feelings of the group.
- Approach people individually and ask for their support.
- Avoid the blame game! When you start to blame someone else for a problem or mistake, catch yourself and instead ask, "How can we fix this together as we move forward?"

Some workers lead by becoming change agents—people who identify, pursue, and implement positive changes in their spheres of influence. Worker Alice Macpherson has this to say about taking initiative by being a change agent: "As a change agent I am committed to change from within myself and my organization and my society. It means that I try to think about the long-term ramifications of the actions and policies of myself and others. I want to be a positive change agent, so I speak up when I see discrimination and I lobby for win-win situations. My organization sees me as someone who can be counted on to speak up, ask questions, and make suggestions. This is not part of my official job description."

Several years ago, John Patrick, a senior strategy executive with IBM in Somers, New York, realized that the Internet would be the future of computing. Soon after his net conversion, Patrick acted independently and quickly. He wrote an IBM internal manifesto called "Get Connected." It identified a number of principles that would reshape industries and reinvent companies, along with the following action items:

- Give every employee an e-mail address.
- Create internal newsgroups.
- Build a corporate web site.

Patrick immediately began to receive memos, phone calls, and e-mail from around the world. Says Patrick, "People didn't know

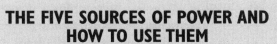

THE FIVE SOURCES OF POWER AND HOW TO USE THEM

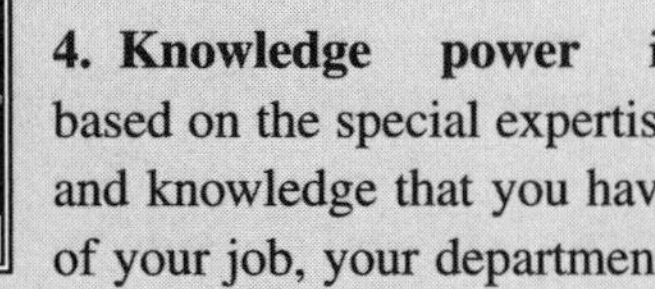

Every employee has five sources of power to draw from. As you prepare to take initiative, assess your potential power sources and use them to your advantage.

1. Personal power is all about your charisma, your passion to achieve, the strength of your convictions, your ability to communicate and inspire, and your leadership skills.

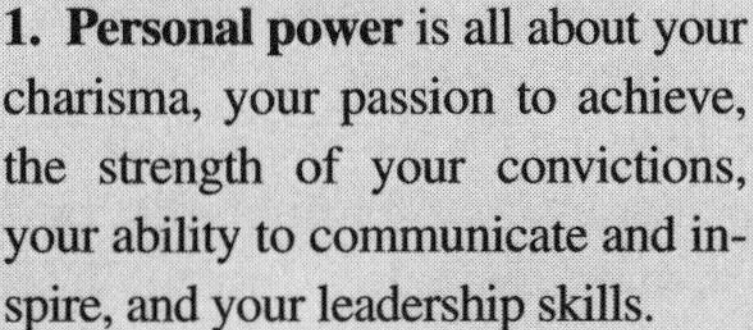

2. Relationship power derives from the network of contacts and friends that you make, develop, and maintain at work. From coworkers who keep you up to date with the goings-on in their part of the organization, to executives who seek you out for special projects—and everyone in between.

3. Position power is directly related to where you reside on your company's organizational chart. Owners, presidents, and CEOs have plenty of position power, while receptionists, clerks, and laborers typically have little or none.

4. Knowledge power is based on the special expertise and knowledge that you have of your job, your department, or your organization. For example, if you're the only one in the company who knows how to bring a dead computer back to life 15 minutes before the FedEx guy is due to pick up that important proposal, you have incredible knowledge power.

5. Task power is inherent in the jobs you are assigned at work. Some work is by nature more important to the health of the organization than others. For example, salespeople, whose job it is to bring in money by selling its products or services, usually have high task power. You can leverage any source of power you have to build your base of power in another source; for instance, you can leverage the relationship power you have from your network of contacts in an organization to obtain increased knowledge power from experts in your network.

where I reported in the company and they didn't care. We shared a common vision that the Internet was going to change everything and that IBM should be a leader." When IBM created a 600-person division to define the company's Internet initiatives a couple of years later, Patrick was named its vice president and chief technology officer.

How many times have you attended a meeting meant to inspire change in an organization, only to have everyone return to business as usual as soon as they get back to their desks? As attendees at the conclusion of a three-day business retreat sponsored by Xaloy, Inc., a manufacturer of bi-metallic cylinders in Pulaski, Virginia, were headed for the door to go home, machinist Roger Roope was committed to not letting *this* meeting suffer a similar fate. "We can't leave now," Roope said. "We have to decide what we're going to do differently on Monday if we expect people to buy in to the need for change." Roope was right. If the individuals who participated in the retreat were to make a real change in the organization, then that change would have to start immediately. Says CEO Walter Cox, "We took Roope's suggestion, regrouped, and searched for a strong, symbolic action that would signal change in a dramatic way. We decided to go back and announce that we were going to remove all the time clocks."

Organizational Change

There are many facets to bringing about organizational change. Here are some of the most important:

- Vision
- Tenacity
- Ability to manage conflict and confront tough situations
- Ability to mobilize others to act
- Strong interpersonal skills
- Technical expertise in the field of organizational change/group dynamics
- Trust and credibility
- A true desire that what is to be done matters and will benefit the collective good

After their company was found legally liable for faulty silicone implants, two employees, Dawn Bartell and Stephanie Burns of Dow Corning in Midland, Michigan, took it upon themselves to organize a show of employee support for the company's management team. Bartell explains, "It was a brainstorm. Stephanie Burns

WHAT MAKES A LEADER?

Anyone in an organization can be a leader. The ability to lead is not a trait formally conferred only on supervisors or managers. In fact, some might say that the most effective leaders in their organizations are informal leaders, line workers without any "official" supervisory or management role. But all leaders must do the following:

- **Inspire action.** Leaders have the ability to inspire those above or below them in the formal hierarchy to take action to achieve a common goal, often far beyond anything those being led could have imagined attaining on their own.

- **Communicate.** Communication is the glue that holds the individuals in an organization together. Great leaders are great communicators. They not only inspire others with their words and deeds but also paint compelling visions of the future, motivating others to follow.

- **Support and facilitate.** Leaders support those with whom they work. They do so by creating an environment that supports individual action and prudent risk taking. Instead of deterring their followers or punishing them for trying to improve products, services, or work processes, they applaud their efforts—loudly and publicly.

Leadership Attributes

In the foreword to *The Leader of the Future,* management guru Peter Drucker lists the following behaviors of any effective leader, including informal leaders:

1. They did not start out with the question "What do I want?" They started out asking, "What needs to be done?"

2. Then they asked, "What can and should I do to make a difference?" This has to be something that both needs to be done and fits the leader's strengths and the way she or he is most effective.

3. They constantly asked, "What are the organization's *mission* and *goals*? What constitutes *performance* and *results* in this organization?"

4. They were extremely tolerant of diversity in people and did not look for carbon copies of themselves. It rarely even occurred to

(continued on next page)

and I were talking about the Operating Committee and what a great job they were doing. We wondered how we could really tell them what we thought. We came to the idea of signatures and then putting it in the newspaper so the community could see it." The brainstorm was a *six*-page advertisement in the *Midland Daily News:* it read, "Dow Corning Management—We're behind you 100%," and was signed by 2,068 employees, contractors, and retirees.

When Gail Seto of Toronto, Ontario, joined The Gap as an assistant manager, she realized that the company's 300-page standard policy-and-procedures manual didn't cover half the issues that come up at a typical store. Instead, new store managers had to learn how to deal with most issues through personal experience, sometimes with less-than-favorable results. Gail knew that there must be a better way to help new managers learn how to run their stores, and she was going to take it upon herself to find it. On her own initiative, Gail drafted a concise training manual that managers could use as a quick and handy guide to running a Gap store. Her manual is now in use in Gap stores throughout Canada.

At IBM's Almaden Research Center in San Jose, California, a dozen young employees are taking initiative to reinvent the way the company does business. Instead of the old-style, buttoned-down-white-collar-and-pinstripe-suit IBM of the past, these employees are forging a new-style, free-spirited, and entrepreneurial IBM where young employees sporting T-shirts, blue jeans, and earrings are the norm. Further evidence of employee-driven change: a pirate flag flies over the cubicle of the team's webmaster; Tekken 2, the Sony PlayStation game, runs on a screen in the conference room; a poster that looks like a ransom note loudly announces, "I cannot be managed by anybody."

Dawn Ross, a former human resources manager for Kentucky Fried Chicken's northwestern U.S. fast-food stores, wanted to help store managers better motivate employees and recognize their efforts, and to reinforce the lessons that store managers learned in KFC's leadership-training program. She hit upon the idea of preparing a leadership-learning newsletter for store managers every month. On her own initiative, and without further approval from her higher-ups, Ross prepared and distributed the one-page newsletter by herself. Not only were the store managers' leadership lessons reinforced, but they appreciated the attention from the corporate office.

When things start to go wrong, many managers fall back on the old ways of doing business: they increase their control over employees and remove them from decision-making roles. However, when Ken Hux was assigned as vice president and general manager of the Sears Licensed Businesses Unit, which licenses

(continued from previous page)

them to ask, "Do I like or dislike this person?" But they were totally—fiendishly—intolerant when it came to a person's *performance, standards,* and *values.*

5. They were not afraid of strength in their associates. They gloried in it. Whether they had heard of it or not, their motto was what Andrew Carnegie wanted to have put on his tombstone: "Here lies a man who attracted better people into his service than he was himself."

6. One way or another, they submitted themselves to the "mirror test"—that is, they made sure that the person they saw in the mirror in the morning was the kind of person they wanted to be, respect, and believe in. This way they fortified themselves against the leader's greatest temptation—to do things that are popular rather than right.

7. Finally, these effective leaders were not preachers; they were *doers.*

Make Good Things Happen

Leaders make good things happen, no matter what position they hold in an organization's formal hierarchy. John Patrick, IBM division vice president, believes that *everyone* in an organization should strive to be a leader and to make good things happen. Here are his tips for doing just that:

1. The less you ask for, the more you can do. Naysayers can't kill projects they don't fund. "Someone would learn about a team and ask, 'Where does it report?'" Patrick says. "Well, it doesn't report to anybody. 'Where's the budget?' There isn't any budget. Nobody could say, 'Let me review your plan.' There wasn't any plan."

2. Just enough is good enough. Want to achieve extraordinary results? Set unreasonable timetables. "Make the calendar your friend," Patrick

(continued on next page)

businesses to sell products and services in retail stores, he decided that maybe it was time to try something different and took the lead.

To counter a crisis-ridden business with declining sales and profits, Hux first experimented with an informal system of allowing workers to participate in decision making. According to Hux, "When I was asked to head the licensing operation, I knew I had to do something different because the business was in a downward spiral in every respect." After witnessing firsthand the benefits of involving nonmanagement employees in decision making, he formalized the process by adopting a program called Goal Sharing, which was based on the tried-and-true principles of the Scanlon Plan (see page 6).

As a result of Hux's taking the reins, which opened a floodgate of employee initiative throughout the organization, the licensing unit became a star performer with double-digit growth and employee turnover was virtually eliminated. Not only that, but the unit consistently records the highest positive attitude scores in the entire Sears organization. Says Hux, "I could never return to traditional management now that I've seen the impact this process can have on an organization."

Utility companies are building a strong record of success in improving their environmental records, often due to employee initiative. At Western Resources, a gas and electric utility headquartered in Topeka, Kansas, a group of environmentally concerned employees approached

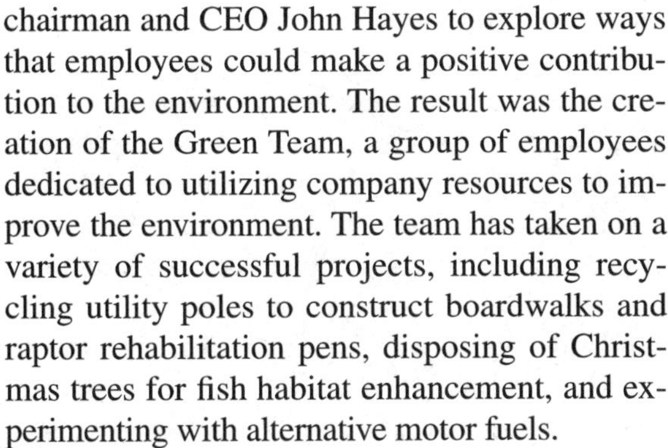

chairman and CEO John Hayes to explore ways that employees could make a positive contribution to the environment. The result was the creation of the Green Team, a group of employees dedicated to utilizing company resources to improve the environment. The team has taken on a variety of successful projects, including recycling utility poles to construct boardwalks and raptor rehabilitation pens, disposing of Christmas trees for fish habitat enhancement, and experimenting with alternative motor fuels.

After noticing that when she met with couples to discuss financial matters, the wives never asked questions, Julia Strayer, vice president at the Private Bank of BankBoston branch in Stamford, Connecticut, took action. Says Strayer, "They're intimidated, so they don't always get the best financial advice." On her own volition, Strayer personally organized and delivered a series of financial seminars to address this knowledge gap. The seminars were very well attended and the bank's female customers were extremely appreciative of Strayer's efforts on their behalf.

When top management threatened to downsize his department, Bill Hewitt, a manager at GTE-Sylvania, was motivated to find solutions that would help the department become more cost-competitive. By recognizing the issues at the heart of the department's financial problems, and by taking initiative to develop and implement a plan to solve them,

(continued from previous page)

says. "Set a date by which something has to happen and work from there. Don't wait until your project is perfect. Get it out and see how people react."

3. Nowhere beats somewhere. "I never put a business-unit name on my card," Patrick says. "People ask me, 'What division do you work for?' It doesn't matter what division I work for. If IBM wins, everyone wins."

4. Lose a teammate, gain a division. Initiative is contagious, and if those who take initiative are spread around an organization, others will follow their example. "I think of it as colonization," Patrick says. "One of our people was just promoted to run marketing for a major division. Somebody said, 'We lost Lee.' We didn't lose Lee, we gained a whole division."

Tactics for Influencing Others

In a recent survey of employees conducted by Gary Yukl and Celcilia Falbe, the following eight tactics were found to be most commonly used to influence others in organizations. Depending on the culture of an organization, some of these tactics may be unacceptable; nonetheless, they are all used often.

1. **Pressure tactics:** making demands, or using threats and intimidation
2. **Upward appeals:** appealing to higher management for assistance or persuading others that the request is approved by upper management
3. **Exchange:** trading one favor for another
4. **Coalitions:** enlisting others to join in with their support
5. **Ingratiation:** building positive sentiments in others through friendliness and charm

(continued on next page)

Hewitt and his department were able to come out on top.

"I was told to reduce my supervisory staff. The thought of losing supervisors who provided day-to-day guidance for the hourly workforce greatly challenged me, and I wondered how I was going to meet company objectives. So I came up with the idea to show people the performance standards that I was measured for: the department's goals and objectives. I used departmental 'white boards' with a green and red marker system. I used green to reflect positive measures and red for negative ones. I took the time to explain to people what the standards were, how they were measured, and the impact on finished-product prices. I also started to track performance, such as labor variance, number of days since last accident, and number of quality rejects, for each department, daily and monthly, to date.

"For the first days and weeks, the performance was typical: some numbers were green; some were red. But because the boards were visible, departments tried to outperform each other. If there were continual 'red days,' we developed low-key problem solving to address any losses. Within months, all the white boards in my departments were green. Over several months, I learned that we were breaking plant records for labor variance and productivity."

For initiative to have an impact throughout an organization, communicating with others is essential. According to Cheryl Babcock of Sarasota, Florida, her ability to communicate well

with her colleagues is part of her success as a change agent who takes initiative to help nudge her organization out of tired, old ways of doing business and into new, more effective ones. "I'm a change agent (and am considered as such by my organization) because I'm willing to spend my time talking, writing, e-mailing, and so on to make other people aware of the paradigm shift that's taking place in my field. I don't always get paid for the time I spend doing that, but I do it anyway. I'll actually go out of my way to do it because I believe so strongly in the process. To be a change agent you need both the ability to talk (in a variety of mediums) so people will at least hear what you are saying and the ability to enlist and show others how to promote the cause. The other thing is passion . . . if you don't have it, nobody else will 'catch' it!"

Sarah was a college student who worked nights and weekends at a swanky waterfront restaurant in Sausalito, California. Because of her desire to ensure that every customer felt welcome and had a pleasant experience at the restaurant, Sarah took advantage of any opportunity to make it a better place. In one case, Sarah noticed that her customers kept asking about the availability of T-shirts, hats, and other novelty items imprinted with the restaurant's name and logo. Although a part-time employee, she went to management and recommended that the company start producing and stocking these potentially popular items for sale. After reviewing the financial data that Sarah independently

(continued from previous page)

6. Rational persuasion: using logical arguments and facts to persuade others

7. Inspirational appeals: using emotionally charged and symbolic language to appeal to another person's sense of loyalty or justice

8. Consultation: seeking another person's participation in decision making and planning

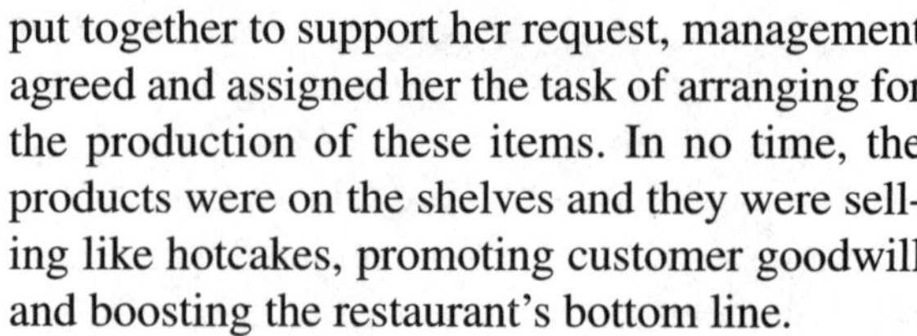

❝Educated risks are the key to success.❞

—William Olsten, CEO, Olsten Services Corp.

put together to support her request, management agreed and assigned her the task of arranging for the production of these items. In no time, the products were on the shelves and they were selling like hotcakes, promoting customer goodwill and boosting the restaurant's bottom line.

Seeing a need to maintain consistency of service to customers, especially "Gold Carders" who thrive on a level of personal service that chain stores usually don't provide, Gail Seto of The Gap in Toronto, Ontario, independently developed a series of workshops on topics such as casual dressing and wardrobe consulting for interested firms in Toronto's financial district. The workshops have been a smashing success, improving customer service and satisfaction.

Impatient with a vendor's presentation on the merits of purchasing an expensive multimedia program, Rick Corry, director of Owens Corning's performance university, had one question for the 200 training executives assembled in the conference room: "Why don't we get together and share what we've got and fund what we need ourselves?" Today, Cory is general manager and CEO of LearnShare in Toledo, Ohio, a unique consortium of leading companies that have pooled their resources to design and produce new training programs. Besides Owens Corning, General Motors, Motorola, Reynolds Metals, and others are members.

Steve Miller, group managing director for the Royal Dutch/Shell Group of Companies, tells a story about a company-sponsored leadership training program. Says Miller, "We had an Austrian team in our first program, and it was clear from the start that it didn't want to be there. During the exercises that we did in the first workshop, out of the six teams participating, the Austrians consistently came in *seventh!* Whatever the exercise was, you could count on the Austrians, individually and collectively, to be last.

"What turned things around was the video exercise. As it happened, the Austrian team leader was called away suddenly, and he wasn't there for the exercise. Now this struggling team was leaderless and facing an 'unconstrained problem': here's your video camera, you've got 90 minutes, go make a video. Good luck! What the team came up with was the story of a guy who has to go to the bathroom very badly. The 'old Shell' video opens with this guy walking cross-legged, in great pain, looking for the men's toilet. He comes to the door marked 'Men,' and it's locked. He goes through a bureaucratic procedure to fill out the form required to open the door. The person he hands the form to has to get it approved by his supervisor. That person rings a bell, and the supervisor comes over and reviews the whole process. Meanwhile, the guy is practically turning green—until he's finally given the key, and he lunges into the men's room. That's the 'old Shell.' Then came the 'new Shell.'

Maximizing Influence

In their book *Influence Without Authority,* authors Allan R. Cohen and David L. Bradford give the following advice for maximizing your influence in an organization:

- Pay attention to what is really important to other members.
- See even those with different interests and expertise as potential allies rather than as adversaries.
- Go out of your way to help others; it builds credits to trade for favors.
- Diagnose the needs of, and take initiative toward, people who won't cooperate; don't view them as enemies and write them off.
- Create win-win results, which lead to a cooperative, trusting environment in which it is easier to make the exchanges needed to get work done through ongoing mutual influence.

> "The best way to predict the future is to invent it."
>
> —Alan Kay, Director of Research, Apple Computer Co.

"The same guy goes to the men's room, but now there's a doorman who ushers him through with a smile. As he goes into a stall, he's handed his own personal roll of toilet paper. When he comes out, he's given his own towel. The service attendant even tries to zip up the guy's fly. The sequence was absolutely hysterical. We showed every team's video and picked the best one. The Austrians won hands down—and that was the beginning of their turnaround. Their leader came back to an energized team, and he began to realize how much talent his team had and how capable his team members were—all along, it was *his* attitude that was getting in the way of his team's creative process. Over the course of the week, they changed the way they worked together. Later, they dramatically improved their business performance in Austria."

LEADERS INFLUENCE ACTIONS

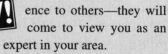

TAKE ACTION NOW!

1. Seek positions of leadership, both formal and informal. Informal leaders often have more power and influence than formal leaders.

2. Set an example. Others will respect your values and naturally look to you for leadership.

3. Become a valuable resource. Offer your expertise and experience to others—they will come to view you as an expert in your area.

4. Be prepared when you present your case. Preparation, or the lack thereof, can make the difference between success and failure when it comes to influencing others.

5. Stick to facts, not emotion. In the long run, facts will win every time.

Communication/ Networking

Today, we have more ways of communicating and networking with one another than ever in the history of the world. In addition to the traditional stalwarts of face-to-face communication, telephones, and written letters, notes, and memos, we have computer e-mail, voice mail, pagers, faxes, cell phones, teleconferencing, and more. However, just because we have all these great ways to stay in touch with one another doesn't mean that they get used—we still have to take the initiative to communicate information that is timely, meaningful, and has purpose to one another, and to build links in our networks with coworkers and others. And despite the dramatic surge in the technology of communication, none of it is worth the circuit board it's transmitted on if the person you are communicating with doesn't understand what you are saying. As Andrew Grove, chairman of Intel Corporation, puts it, "How well we communicate is not determined by how well we say things but by how well we are understood."

When Ann Maurutto, a manager at SSM Health Care in St. Louis, Missouri, heard employees complain among themselves about problems with their laptops, she posted large sheets of paper in the cafeteria labeled "Problems" and "Solutions" and encouraged employees to post and answer each other's questions. The idea worked like a charm. Not only did her act of initiative help employees solve their

> "People with initiative are always looking out for fresh ideas, willing to take on challenges and learn new things."
>
> —Juliet, from the Internet

Taking Initiative in Meetings

1. Really listen to what others have to say.
2. Participate actively in the discussion, but don't dominate it.
3. Prepare for the meeting.
4. Reflect the strength of your own convictions by speaking clearly and loudly enough for all to hear.
5. Help keep the meeting on topic and on time.

computer problems, but it opened up a new channel of communication among employees within the organization.

Jim Jordano, manager of investment analysis at Sikorsky Aircraft, makes every effort to understand his customers' problems. He takes the initiative to ask them exactly what they need and when they need it. This process often results in significant time savings and limits his workweek to about 50 hours. The result? With the extra time, Jordano is able to spend less time at the office and to help raise his three children. He even found enough time to complete his MBA.

Great managers understand that the freedom to fail and try again is an important element in unleashing employee initiative. In an effort to transform a slow-moving, customer-unfriendly bureaucracy into a fast-moving, customer-friendly service organization, a vice president at Alagasco, a natural gas distributor headquartered in Birmingham, Alabama, distributed "Get out of jail, free!" cards to his entire staff. When employees make mistakes in their attempts to deliver outstanding service, they go to the vice president, discuss what they have learned from the experience, turn in a card, and are immediately forgiven. Then, before they leave, the vice president hands them another "Get out of jail, free!" card to be used later. This simple but effective program not only improved communication between workers and management but spurred a huge

surge in employee initiative, resulting in a complete turnaround in the quality of service delivery to Alagasco customers.

Hewlett-Packard's Lauren Martin takes her approach to personal networking beyond the borders of the company. Martin joined HP in 1984 as an accounting clerk. Today she runs a career self-reliance program for the organization. How does Martin learn about the projects she wants to work on? "Once or twice a month, I have lunch with an industry peer," she says. "I make it a point to strike up relationships with people who do the kind of business I do or am interested in. In the past, people focused on their direct relationship with their manager. In a project environment, people need strong, healthy relationships with their peers." That's just as true of peers inside the company as of those outside. Martin emphasizes, "I always assume that the people working with me on a project may someday manage me. Or that I may manage them. So I treat people with that in mind. I always cultivate a social relationship—'Let's have lunch and talk.'"

A forward-thinking manager at the Mirage Hotel in Las Vegas initiated a simple two-way activity to encourage communication between management and staff. Every month the manager asks her staff, "What one thing can I do better for you this month?" After listening and noting the employees' ideas, the manager then

Communicate Early and Often

- Make it personal if it's important.
- Choose the best time for maximum impact.
- More communication is not necessarily better communication.
- Say what you need, before someone else decides for you.
- Take risks expressing your opinions before a decision is made. Once it's made, fully support it—even if you don't agree with it.
- Develop and leverage an active network of relationships within your organization.
- Join or attend professional associations and participate in available corporate training.
- At the end of each day, update your files with any new people you've met and in what context.
- Share your ideas with others.

> “As it becomes bigger, the tendency of a corporation is to create pockets of bureaucracy that love to write memorandums. I'm just not a memo writer. I like to look someone in the eye and say, ‘Let's talk.’”
>
> —Peter L. Scott, Chairman, Emhart Corp.

tells her staff, “Great, and here is one thing that all of you can do better for us this month.” This technique builds connections between all employees while focusing on continuous improvement.

Taking initiative by cold calling and networking with potential clients is a tried-and-true way for salespeople of all kinds to build business. An editor for a business magazine tells this story about a recruiter who called her out of the blue and gained an earnest client in the process. “A woman who ran a recruiting company for technical writers interviewed me for potential job opportunities that she had available. As I explained my background, she became more and more impressed with what I'd done. She helped me revise my résumé to more clearly reflect my capabilities and talents. I went into the interview with the recruiter unsure whether I wanted to work with her and came out completely sold on her and what she could do for me. What she did, effectively, is affirm my talents and capabilities. That made me trust her and get excited about the opportunities she told me about. I wondered to myself if all recruiters do this kind of ‘self-esteem building’ and, if so, how incredibly effective it must be. I hadn't had a nice word from my direct supervisors for six years—and an awful lot of harsh ones. All of a sudden, someone was telling me I was talented and worthwhile and very valuable to an employer. Wow!”

HOW TO GET OTHERS TO HELP YOU

BE YOUR OWN BOSS

Inevitably, as you try to take initiative you will need the help of others. Getting this help may have less to do with your formal position and authority and more to do with your strategy and approach, which can range from a simple favor to convincing others to accept a priority of yours as if it were their own. Here are some guidelines:

■ **Define what needs to be done.** The more you can identify specifically the help you need and the tasks to be done, the better. Fuzzy goals lead to fuzzy results. By defining all the tasks required, you increase the likelihood of success. Be sure to include status reports and deadlines as you define specific action items that are needed.

■ **Ask an individual for help.** When you make a general request for volunteers during a meeting, workers often interpret it as "Whoever doesn't have much of anything to do can work on this." Your chances of getting someone to volunteer thus tend to be slim. However, if you think about who might best be able to help with a task and then specifically ask that person for help, your odds of getting him or her to accept the task increase dramatically. For example, "John, I'm putting together a team to assess if we should purchase or lease the new equipment we need in our department, and I would like you to be a part of the team. We need your expertise in financial analysis to make the right decision—can we count on you to join us?"

■ **Thank others for their assistance.** Thank and acknowledge others for their help. The person will feel that his or her time and energy were appreciated. In addition, you will likely be able to call on the person again in the future for assistance. People are glad to help those who appreciate their efforts.

If you limit yourself to only the things you can do, your results will also be limited. If you have a good idea, think it through and show others how they can help achieve the desired result.

One Man's Brainstorming

As director of marketing promotions for SmithKline Beecham, the global pharmaceutical giant based in Philadelphia, Scott Dever is always on the lookout for new ways to expand the market for the company's vaccines and antibiotics. His approach: gather a few of his colleagues to brainstorm ideas, then seek out resources to turn those ideas into full-fledged projects.

"The most valuable projects are those initiated at the grassroots level," he argues. "Lots of people can take someone else's idea and make it happen. But if you're tuned in enough to what's going to make your company successful into the next century, you can contribute on a totally different level."

Knowing the importance of networking when starting a new job, Eileen Burke, senior vice president at Fleet Financial Group in New York City, made it her first priority. Within 30 days of her hire, Burke took the initiative to call her counterparts in Boston to schedule a series of informal meetings. During the course of one of these meetings, she learned a critical bit of advice about her boss, that he responds to spoken requests more readily when they are accompanied by concise memos. According to Burke, "That tip took the guesswork out of figuring out how best to communicate with my boss." And it shows that you just never know what kinds of good things are going to happen when you take initiative.

Looking for work for her recently formed consulting firm, Patti Koltnow knew that new clients weren't going to just walk in the door; she would have to seek them out. Koltnow used the *Women's Yellow Pages* to make targeted telephone calls to invite a group of successful career women to network with one another over a relaxed lunch. As the result of one such lunch, the director of the USC Orange County campus offered Koltnow a contract as a marketing consultant for the school's mini-MBA program for women.

The importance of keeping in touch with coworkers cannot be overemphasized, especially when one is not a part of the formal meeting routines of an organization. As a former Wall Street mergers-and-acquisitions analyst, Brian Graham knows what it's like to put in an extraordinary number of hours at work. However, now that he has three children and has begun to put more emphasis on the quality of his life away from the office, Graham makes a point to find shortcuts at work wherever he can. Graham skips routine meetings, thus freeing himself up to work uninterrupted, but he stays in the loop by asking his coworkers for information. Says Graham, "The key for me is to know what *not* to do, and to always be looking for the path of quickest resolution."

> "I think of creativity as civilized tenacity. You have to defend your ideas, educate your colleagues, and recruit allies. You also have to be willing to rethink and revise."
>
> —Clar Evans, Director, Creative Advisory Group, Hallmark Cards, Inc.

Making a presentation in an interesting and innovative way can make the message much more vibrant, and its chance of being received by your audience much higher. A team participating in a three-day retreat for bi-metallic cylinder producer Xaloy, Inc., of Pulaski, Virginia, did just that. The team galloped into the presentation room on broomstick horses dressed in authentically designed Confederate uniforms. Their novel approach was a complete surprise even to CEO Walter Cox and added interest and excitement to their presentation. An employee playing General Robert E. Lee called upon each of his officers and troops to give reports. The team interviewed salespeople and customers and reviewed trade magazines. They presented an overview of the market, competitors, and comparative strengths and weaknesses, as well as other important data. Says

> “I want workers to go home at night and say ‘I built that car.’”
>
> —PEHR G. GYLLENHAMMAR, Chairman, Volvo

Cox, “Their presentation was excellent. They did it in a funny, creative way and it was right on the mark. It was especially impressive because none of the members were in sales and marketing. All but one were in manufacturing.”

HOW TO HAVE INFLUENCE IN MEETINGS

The whole point of having a meeting is to obtain the best ideas and opinions from everyone who attends. If you don't speak up and get your ideas across to others, then no one gains anything by attending. Here are some simple ways to make an impact on meetings, according to Roger Mosvich and Bob Nelson in their book *We Have to Start Meeting Like This*:

1. State the idea you wish the group to consider. “I'm not sure we should adopt that conclusion so quickly.”

2. Relate the significance of the idea to the previous statement. “A recent *Fortune* survey seems to directly contradict what was just said about the values of American businessmen . . .”

3. Support the idea with adequate evidence. “There are three key findings that stand out in this poll of top American business executives . . .” (Cite the three pieces of evidence and draw a conclusion.)

4. Integrate the comment into the discussion by asking the group to respond to the statement. “This information seems to be equally valid but it is in conflict with some of our group's findings. I think it qualifies our previous conclusion a great deal. Do you all agree with that statement?”

At Bread Loaf Construction Company in Middlebury, Vermont, an innovative idea to better link the field and corporate offices came not from management but from an employee who decided to take initiative. Leo Breshnahan, a field worker, approached executive vice president John Leehman at the company's annual meeting for its 160 employees and complained, "We do all the work out in the field, while people in the office are just having a good time." Leehman decided to respond to Breshnahan's issue by inviting him to spend a day seeing how the office crew earned its living. According to Leehman, "It was a real turning point for Breshnahan. He knows where he can go in the system to get what he needs to do his job better and so do other employees who have followed in his footsteps." Now, an employee is selected each month to tour the corporate offices and construction sites to get a better idea of exactly what people do and how they can be of help.

Five Meeting Don'ts

1. Don't invite people to attend unless they really need to be there.
2. Don't meet without an agenda.
3. Don't start late.
4. Don't get off the subject.
5. Don't tolerate excessive interruptions.

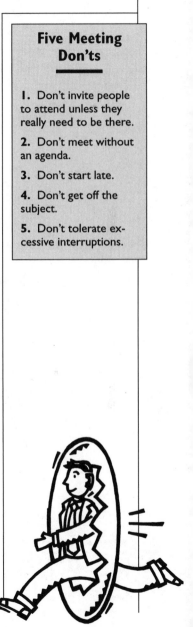

At Going Places, a British travel agency in the United Kingdom, one of the most far-reaching innovations has been a consultative forum for the company's 5,000 employees—a forum initiated and attended by regular employees to discuss their concerns and share information. The meetings, held six times a year and chaired by managing director Tony Bennett but not open to line managers, have aired a wide variety of worker issues, from the lackluster state of some shops to the right of

> “Initiative gives me signs of employee intelligence and inspiration.”
>
> —MUHSEN, from the Internet

women employees to wear uniform trousers. Other innovations suggested by Going Places staff during these meetings and then taken up by management have included a £1 million investment in fridges, cooking facilities, and better seating for shop staff whose busiest periods are lunchtimes. The forum has had a clear and positive effect on all aspects of a business that, says Bennett, “had previously neither encouraged staff to be innovative nor had thought of rewarding them for being so.”

Managers at a division of aerospace manufacturer Lockheed Martin Missiles and Space Company in Sunnyvale, California, initiated weekly, one-hour “Manager Only Meetings” to improve communication and coordination of efforts. According to one manager, “The ‘Manager Only Meetings’ have been a most successful way to get in touch with the kinds of problems and things going on in the labs that we don’t necessarily hear about because we’re so involved in the day-to-day activities of running our own department.”

Taking initiative to bring a human touch to a program helps everyone who participates to get more out of it. While working as the project manager of an orientation meeting for the business faculty at the University of Victoria in Victoria, British Columbia, Janice Seto took the initiative to create an extra-special closing ceremony. Rather than just the usual

congratulations and handshake, Seto presented each teacher who came forward to the podium with a box of special chocolates and a handwritten thank-you note. The participants were particularly moved when they later discreetly compared thank-you notes and found that each one was different. Says Seto, "Too often we get word-processed notes where the space for NAME has been filled in to lessen the generic quality of the message. This doesn't work at all! Plus, the scarcity of handwritten notes makes the ones you do get more precious. It says hey, someone cared enough to spend three minutes on me, as opposed to the word-processed note that takes only three seconds of somebody's time." People appreciate it when someone takes the initiative to do something special for them.

> "To manage your boss you've got to set reasonable expectations, communicate honestly, and use humor to defuse conflict."
>
> —DEIRDRE POLSON, Director of Marketing, HomeShark, Inc.

As an accounting student at Mount Mary College in Milwaukee, Wisconsin, Kerry Poznanski decided to arrange an internship before she graduated for two reasons. "I wanted to get some practical experience before I graduated, and I also wanted to meet people in the profession and begin to build a network," she said. She accepted an internship with the firm of Conley McDonald LLP in Brookfield, Wisconsin, with the idea of preparing for her future. "There was no guarantee of a job after graduation, but I thought this would be a good way to start building a list of contacts in the industry." Poznanski ended up staying on with the firm as a tax team associate after graduation. She

recommends that students start exploring fields they are interested in as soon as possible. "By getting out and introducing yourself to people and finding what opportunities are out there, you get a better idea of what you can do when you graduate," she said.

COMMUNICATION AND NETWORKING TIPS

TAKE ACTION NOW!

1. Improve the quality, not just the quantity, of your communication. More communication is not necessarily better communication.

2. Communicate sooner rather than later. Don't wait for problems to occur—head them off before they have a chance to develop.

3. Find out the way each person prefers to communicate. Some people communicate best on the phone, others face-to-face or via e-mail.

4. Don't be a slave to your desk. Meet and network with others on their own turf.

5. Keep up with technology. There are more ways to communicate than ever before. Stay on top of the latest developments.

Managing Up

The word *management* brings to mind visions of bosses dictating down to their subordinates. However, management isn't limited to this old-fashioned view of how to get things done in an organization. Workers can push their own innovative ideas, opinions, and decisions *up* the organization, and help their supervisors and managers do a better job. In fact, a study conducted by Sidney Yoshiba for Ford Motor Company's British Columbia division found that only 4 percent of the problems in an organization could be identified by senior management: when middle management, all supervisors, and all staff were factored in, this proportion increased to 9 percent, 74 percent, and 100 percent, respectively. There is plenty of room for employees at all levels of an organization to help their supervisors and managers do a better job, and to improve the performance of their organizations in the process. Here's another tip: empathy plays a big part in your ability to effectively manage up. Keep in mind that your boss may be under more stress and pressure from above (and below) than you realize. A sincere, specific, and timely message that says you appreciate a particular behavior, such as your boss's openness or integrity, goes a long way toward reinforcing the very behavior you value—making for a better workplace for everyone. Master the skill of managing up, and you'll have much greater control over your own destiny—both on and off the job.

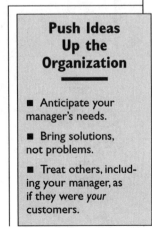

Push Ideas Up the Organization

- Anticipate your manager's needs.
- Bring solutions, not problems.
- Treat others, including your manager, as if they were *your* customers.

Bill Taylor, regional team leader for CP Corporation in San Jose, California, had a new employee tell him, "Once a month I'm going to

Designing Your Goals

Planning and persistence are key factors in ensuring that the goals you set will be achieved. Here are some things to consider as you design your goals:

- Determine in advance the benefits of your goals, to yourself and to the organization.
- Be prepared to sell others on the benefits of your goals.
- Don't be afraid to enlist others to help you achieve your goals.
- Be patient but persistent as you work toward your goals.
- Believe in yourself, and in your ability to attain your goals.

come into your office and tell you about all the great things I've been doing. You're going to agree with me because I need to hear that from you." After about six months, at the end of one such meeting, the employee announced: "You're getting good at this!" Taylor had to agree, because he never took time to thank or praise employees before.

Kentucky Housing Corporation (KHC), the state housing finance agency and a public, self-supporting corporation located in Frankfort, Kentucky, has a charitable leave policy that offers employees paid time off to work on housing-related projects. This charitable leave allows KHC employees, many of whom are restricted to in-house responsibilities, to gain hands-on experience working side-by-side with housing recipients and other housing providers, reap the rewards of helping people with housing needs, and become more in touch with the families who benefit from their office work.

The idea of granting charitable leave was originally conceived by a KHC employee who had volunteered personal time to help build homes for less fortunate families. Realizing the benefits to the individuals, the community, and the agency, this staff member conveyed to management the many advantages of volunteering for charitable housing endeavors. Management then recommended, with success, that the KHC board of directors adopt a charitable leave policy.

"Thanks to this policy," said one of KHC's

employee volunteers, "we have the opportunity to experience firsthand the impact affordable housing programs can have on the families we serve." A majority of KHC employees have volunteered to assist with charitable housing endeavors and, as a result, have helped build homes at several locations throughout Kentucky and in Los Angeles, Houston, and Mexico. Employees who have volunteered in the past are eager to return to a construction site, and those who have not yet experienced the rewards wait anxiously for the next opportunity.

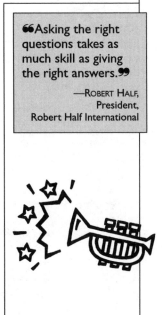

> "Asking the right questions takes as much skill as giving the right answers."
>
> —Robert Half, President, Robert Half International

Andrea Rosen, sales and marketing manager for Living Language, an imprint of Random House Inc. in New York City, prides herself on how she takes initiative at work. While it's not always easy, Rosen finds that, in the end, her efforts have proved to be successful and productive for both her and her organization. She has used one strategy in particular over the years when preparing for her annual performance reviews. Says Rosen, "Often employees go into their reviews and assume that they will receive the percentage raise allotted. Good attendance is only one component of the review! My belief is that you are in control of your raise/review all year long and you must take steps to prove your worth!" Rosen achieved this by keeping a journal. Every Friday she would take a few moments to write down valid points that occurred during the week, anything from a big sale she made to a customer to an important point or suggestion

that she raised in a meeting. Rosen continues, "I called it 'My Success Journal.' It's the greatest thing to do because there's no way you can remember all of your accomplishments! Longevity at a job doesn't get you ahead or earn for you the deserved recognition; a well-thought-out plan and list of your accomplishments do."

"We know what happens to people who stay in the middle of the road. They get run over."

—ANEURIN BEVAN, (1897–1960), English Labour Leader and Minister of Health

---

HOW TO SAY NO: A STORY

BE YOUR OWN BOSS

An important aspect about being your own boss is control over your most valuable asset: your time. You need to guard your time wisely to ensure that it is used mainly in pursuit of the goals and activities that are important to *you*. People who don't stand up for themselves are bound to be used by those around them who do.

Do you ever have a hard time saying no to others? Many people do. When someone asks them to do something as a favor, they figure that the person making the request must have a good reason for asking and they seek to comply. They reason it was a compliment to be asked and you never know when you might need a favor in return.

People who can't say no end up constantly scrambling to finish their commitments to others, often denying their own priorities, including family and friends.

My turning point came when my life insurance policy changed agents. The new agent called and asked if I could meet with her the following week, on Wednesday or Thursday. After checking my calendar and seeing I had time available on those days I answered, "Sure." When I found myself in a crunch on the day of the appointment, I called to see if it was possible to the meet the following week. When she said fine, I felt the

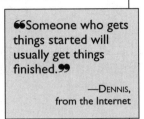

According to Marsha Shade, administrative assistant at Baudville, Inc., a producer of team-building software, papers, and accessories located in Grand Rapids, Michigan, one way employees can determine what ideas and solutions to push up the organization to management is to "pretend" that the company or business they are working for belongs to them.

> "Someone who gets things started will usually get things finished."
>
> —DENNIS, from the Internet

agent was doing me an incredible favor. Then it happened again and, half-embarrassed and half-guilty, I begged for another schedule change.

As I hung up, I thought: "What am I doing? Why am I bending over backward to accommodate this person I don't even know, just because she asked to meet with me? Why am I letting a stranger control my time?"

I called back and promptly took the offensive: What did the agent want to meet about? Was it necessary to meet face-to-face? How much time did she need? I listened and decided to be firm: "I'm sorry, but I've got too much going on right now to meet with you," I said. "Would next month be a better time to get together?" the agent countered. "No," I said, standing up for myself. "Let me just plan to call you if I need something."

When someone asks you to do something, don't ask yourself, "Do I have time?" because if you go out far enough on your calendar you'll be able to find some white space. Instead, ask yourself, "Is this really important to me?" And if it's not—don't do it!

Granted, if the request comes from your boss, you may not have as much leeway as when it comes from an acquaintance or a colleague. Still, you don't have to automatically say yes. Explain what you have going on and let your boss decide if what he wants you to do is more or less important than your current priorities. He may even help you delegate one of your projects to someone else.

Stand up for yourself and your priorities—and in the process reclaim your life!

Managing Your Boss

According to writer Marie-Jeanne Julliand, there are five key ways to manage your boss:

1. Offer solutions, not complaints. Whining about a problem or blaming someone else for it just puts your boss on the defensive. Instead, tell your boss you recognize that he or she has external pressures, and then offer a solution that works for both of you.

2. Apologize. If you make a mistake, admit you are wrong. "It's extremely powerful and disarming for managers, as it's so rarely done," says Stanford business professor and author Jeffrey Pfeffer. After the apology, take up the subject again in the productive way suggested above.

3. Stay central in the information flow. Make a point of being up-to-date in the areas for which your boss needs information.

(continued on next page)

The difference in perspective that comes from a "the-company-belongs-to-me" attitude encourages each employee to see him- or herself as crucial to the success of the business.

Self-motivating thoughts like "If I owned this company I would . . ." or "If I was in charge I could . . ." can lead an employee to research a project or task and make constructive suggestions for change. Thinking and acting as if "the company belongs to me" encourages an employee to dream big, to pay attention to detail, and to see beyond his or her own area of the business and consider the company's "big picture." If "the company belongs to me" as an employee, I have much to gain by making sure the way I do my job helps "my company" to succeed.

Managing up can be as simple as making the right point to management at the right time and place. At a recent staff meeting, Jennifer Lawton, CEO of Net Daemons Associates, Inc. in Woburn, Massachusetts, announced that she planned to grow the company 100 to 200 percent in the next year. While this kind of growth may have sounded like a terrific goal for the company's CEO, some of the company's employees, who would be burdened by working extremely long hours under severe stress and with strained resources, were less than enthusiastic. Concerned with the negative impact that growth of this magnitude could have on the organization, an engineer took initiative and questioned the figure. Lawton talked to

staff at great length about her estimate and eventually lowered the projection to 80 to 100 percent growth. Says Lawton about the change, "His question caused me to think about how that growth feels from an engineer's perspective." Lawton decided to grow the company more slowly rather than risk alienating her employees.

When her husband told her he wanted to move to Knoxville, Tennessee, to help grow his family's business, a year-round Christmas retail store catering to Smoky Mountain tourists, Carolyn Fairbank, a program manager for American Management Systems (AMS) in Fairfax, Virginia, made a proposal to her boss. She wanted to stay with the company and would set up a home office in Knoxville and continue to work for AMS as a telecommuter, using a telephone, a fax, and a PC hooked electronically to the home office. Her boss agreed. Now, instead of watching her career suffer because she'd pulled herself out of the organizational mainstream, Fairbank has steadily ascended the AMS corporate ladder through good old-fashioned hard work and an ability to work effectively and independently from her home office. Now senior principal of AMS's financial service practice, she received her second major promotion the same month she moved to Tennessee.

When John Rogener, program director for Citicorp/Citibank's transaction services

(continued from previous page)

This will give you a leg up in your relationship.

4. Praise your boss. Giving *genuine* compliments can reap surprising rewards.

5. Build alliances. Other managers in the organization may be able to serve as mentors and give you valuable information on how to approach your boss.

How to Manage Your Manager

Managing one's manager is an essential skill for any employee to learn and master. Lois Frankel, author of *Overcoming Your Strengths: 8 Reasons Why Successful People Derail and How to Get Back on Track*, gives her clients the following tips for managing up within their organizations:

- Make giving feedback to you easy by asking the boss every few months for two or three things that you can do to improve your performance.
- Critically assess what the boss asks you to do and make suggestions for ways to improve on the initial idea.
- View differences with the boss as just that—not confrontations to be won or lost.
- Don't surprise the boss. Keep him or her informed of major changes to plans before others begin talking about them.

(continued on next page)

training department, was directed by management to train 1,700 employees in object-oriented technology, he sensed that the training would not be effective; the employees would not learn the things that they needed to get their jobs done. Rogener came up with what he considered to be a better way and presented it up the organizational chain of command. Instead of training 1,700 employees all at once, Rogener convinced management to change the program's mission and to support his plan for varied and smaller-scale training and development support services to his clients, with excellent results. Says Rogener, "What's the bottom line? You have to believe in yourself. You must be responsible for your own decisions rather than letting the institution dictate to you."

Although the banking industry is well known for its conservatism, Brian Bush, an employee in BankBoston's Corporate Banking branch in Hartford, Connecticut, thought it would be beneficial to his bank if it supported a socially progressive cause. He convinced his employer to sponsor the 1997 Connecticut Pride Festival, a celebration of Connecticut's lesbian, gay, bisexual, and transgendered community and friends. The bank agreed, thereby reinforcing its commitment to reach out to all members of the diverse community in which it does business, and generating many new customers through its sponsorship.

At United Electric Controls in Watertown, Massachusetts, Harry Moumdjian has been building—and rebuilding—diaphragm assemblies for the past 16 years. He wanted to find a way to cut down the number of faulty assemblies that came back from the inspection department, not only to reduce the amount of reworking he would personally have to perform, but also to save the company time and money. "They always found leaks," Moumdjian says. He made his supervisor an offer and convinced him it was the right thing to do: "Let me do the testing," he said, "and I'll give you a 100 percent leak-free guarantee." With the help of the company's model shop, Moumdjian set about building an aquarium big enough to hold one of his diaphragm assemblies. To test an assembly, he figured he could simply run an air hose through it, then stand back and check for air bubbles. The sole sticking point: finding a way to position the assembly so he could see it from every angle. "Once we got that, it was very nice," says Moumdjian. "I can tell exactly where the leak is coming from, so I can fix it." With the change, the number of faulty assemblies leaving his department has dramatically decreased, giving Moumdjian more time to focus on other priorities.

Ashley Korenblat, former president of Merlin Manufacturing, a Cambridge, Massachusetts–based bike manufacturer, decided to redesign the rear brakes on the company's rugged road bikes. She was certain that the new design

(continued from previous page)

- Remember and abide by the Golden Rule of Management: he or she who has the gold sets the rules.
- Before giving feedback to the boss, weigh the potential career risk versus the potential profit.
- Consistently beat the deadlines that the boss assigns to you.
- Separate the image of the boss from that of your father or mother: you may be responding to him or her from past experiences with authority, not in the present.

> “Even the most sincere and effective leadership can never empower a single employee. True empowerment—and the only lasting kind—must be brought about by the employees themselves. Leaders most certainly have a role to play: They must open doors and encourage, but ultimately the best help they can give involves staying out of the way.”
>
> —Joan Lloyd, Columnist

would be cheaper because it didn't involve expensive welding, and Merlin could subcontract out the work during a period in which it was otherwise extremely busy. Korenblat gave the go-ahead to start production. Shortly after the first order was placed, her purchasing agent, realizing the new design was faulty, approached Korenblat and insisted that she reconsider her decision. Korenblat allows, "I probably wasn't very successful at disguising my impatience." After taking another look, however, it turned out that the new design was going to lead to a new series of expenses that added up to a lot more than a little extra welding time. By taking the initiative to push Korenblat to review her decision, the purchasing agent helped the company avoid a costly mistake. Says Korenblat, "I had to admit I'd been just plain wrong. That employee's persistence saved us a lot of money."

Janice Seto's father always bought whole milk for her family's restaurant, The Coronation in Bowmanville, Ontario. One day, Janice noticed that 2 percent milk was cheaper and suggested to her father that they give it a try. Her father said, "No, 2 percent milk isn't going to make the pies turn out as well." One day Janice took it upon herself to order 2 percent milk without telling her father about it. She continued to do so for about a month, and then she let the cat out of the bag. By then, the results spoke for themselves—the restaurant's pies were still great, and the change saved a lot of money as well.

Within 90 days of being hired, Stewart Gray, a technical support specialist at Baudville, Inc., a paper products catalog retailer based in Grand Rapids, Michigan, was asked to test an updated version of an existing piece of software using a loose set of guidelines supplied by management. He decided not to limit himself to those guidelines, and took it upon himself to provide feedback about all aspects of the application. He let his department manager know how he felt about the updated version of the software, and what he thought could improve it—much to his boss's delight. Within a few weeks, Gray attended the monthly company meeting and bonuses were announced. Much to his surprise, he received a very generous bonus. Says Gray, "That token of appreciation motivated me to continue taking initiative wherever I could make a difference with new viewpoints and ideas."

Developing a Strong Working Relationship with Your Boss

- Take action on potential problems before they become real problems.
- Be willing to take on new challenges.
- Don't be a "yes" man or "yes" woman. Communicate diplomatically, but frankly and honestly, at all times.
- Don't try to hide bad news.
- Anticipate the needs of your organization and your boss, and act on them.

Janet Perez, a writer for Metro Source, a radio news network based in Scottsdale, Arizona, was sure that changing from the traditional eight-hours-a-day/five-days-a-week schedule to a ten-hours-a-day/four-days-a-week schedule would not only make her more efficient but would be a definite benefit to her organization. Because Metro Source operates 24 hours a day, the traditional eight-hours-a-day schedule meant that there was no overlap of shifts: as one shift was leaving, another one was arriving. This situation was not conducive to a smooth handoff of news and information from shift to

shift. Perez convinced her boss to give it a try, and her plan was put into effect. Sure enough, by overlapping shifts, Perez was able to dramatically improve communication between shifts. Now Metro Source offers a ten-hours-a-day/ four-days-a-week schedule as an option for all employees.

> "An idiot with initiative will accomplish more in a week than a genius talking about an idea with his friends for a year."
>
> —MARTIN, from the Internet

SECRETS TO MANAGING UP

TAKE ACTION NOW!

1. Make your boss look like a hero. The better job you do, the better your department—and your boss—will look to corporate higher-ups.

2. Don't be shy. Tell your boss what's on your mind—don't make him or her guess.

3. Be proactive. Anticipate problems and solve them at your level, before they become bigger problems that only your boss can solve.

4. Be your own best advocate. Learn how to present a clear and compelling case for what you want, whether it's a raise or a promotion, an increase in responsibility or authority, or something else you want your boss to do for you. Support your case with hard facts and evidence, not emotion.

5. Enlist others to help. There is strength in numbers. The more people you can bring around to your point of view, the better chance you'll have to see it implemented.

Working in Teams

Employee teams have been credited with everything from preventing labor unrest to saving organizations countless billions of dollars. However, while teams *can* be a key factor in the success of any organization, just putting employees into teams is no guarantee that any productive work will occur. In fact, many teams, especially those to whom management refuses to grant any significant amount of authority or autonomy, end up wasting countless hours and dollars coming up with ideas that are promptly placed on a shelf or filed away in a drawer, never to see the light of day. The secret to effective teams is *initiative:* employees who are willing to work together with the other members of their teams to make a real difference in their organizations. As David Ehlen, chief executive officer of Wilson Learning, a management training firm in Eden Prairie, Minnesota, put it, advancement in the new world of business teams "is measured not only by your individual contributions, but by how effective you are as a collaborative team member."

Be a Team Spirit Player

- Have clear rules and expectations.
- Agree upon your purpose.
- Compromise to make progress.
- Listen more than you talk.
- Be cheerful about helping out.
- Volunteer for challenging or unusual assignments.
- Go out of your way to help coworkers by volunteering to fill in for them when they are sick or on vacation.

Bill Lorntson and a small group of coworkers at BI Performance Services, an incentive product and services company in Minneapolis, Minnesota, became concerned that traveling associates might be wasting money and affecting the company's bottom line when they made long-distance phone calls to pick up their e-mail messages. The employees decided that the

> “There is a difference between attacking a decision and attacking the man who made the decision.”
>
> —Maurice S. Trotter, New York University

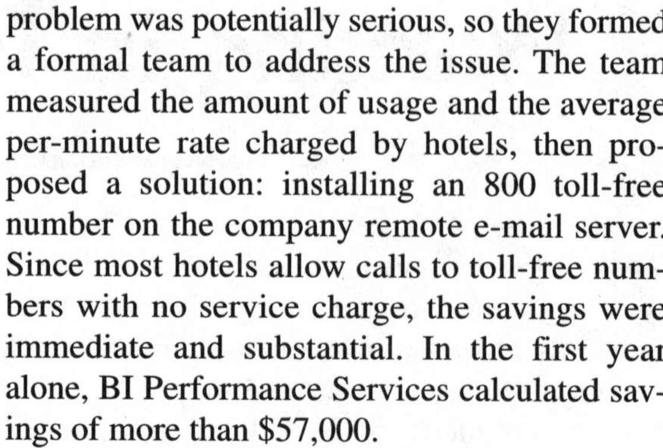

problem was potentially serious, so they formed a formal team to address the issue. The team measured the amount of usage and the average per-minute rate charged by hotels, then proposed a solution: installing an 800 toll-free number on the company remote e-mail server. Since most hotels allow calls to toll-free numbers with no service charge, the savings were immediate and substantial. In the first year alone, BI Performance Services calculated savings of more than $57,000.

St. Mary’s Health Center in St. Louis, Missouri, recently underwent a complete, top-to-bottom renovation. As part of the renovation, an entirely new emergency room (ER) was designed and built. However, instead of assigning this task to an outside design firm, a team of ER employees volunteered to design the new ER themselves. During the year-long process, the employees solicited input from patients, constructed room mock-ups complete with full-size cutouts of equipment that could be moved around to test different floor configurations, and tried out every single piece of equipment before okaying it for final placement. According to Marianne Fournie, clinical director of the emergency department for St. Mary’s Health Center, “It’s been four years since we built the new emergency room, and there’s not a single thing our staff would change about it.” Because the ER was designed around the emergency process, instead of the other way around, St. Mary’s offers a much-improved environment for its

patients *and* its employees. The new ER has knocked a whopping 100 minutes off the average patient visit, and the employee team that designed it received a Missouri Quality Team Award from the state of Missouri in 1997.

A glove manufacturer's customer wanted pairs of gloves shrink-wrapped. However, a custom-built shrink-wrap station would cost several thousand dollars—far too much to justify—and it would be hard to install (getting the temperature correct so that the gloves were not damaged). A team of workers proposed building their own. Working with a plant engineer, the team took locally available parts (a small motor, range eye cover pans, and a paint heat-stripping gun—all available at local retailers) and built a turntable-mounted shrink-wrap station. Cost of this example of employees working together to take initiative to improve their workplace? Less than $100.

One civil engineering unit of the Tennessee Valley Authority (TVA) was responsible for checking about 100 warning sirens at a nuclear plant every month. The task required monitoring each siren with sensitive electronic equipment to verify that each had indeed sounded. When a second plant opened nearby during a hiring freeze, the same group was required to check a total of 205 sirens in the same period of time (105 more than their usual quota). On their own initiative, the team developed a work schedule

“You can be very smart but that won't get you far if you don't show that you have ideas, that you can problem solve, that you will take the bull by the horns when you need to and just take care of things.”

—Cynthia, from the Internet

DECIDING WHAT'S IMPORTANT

Whenever you decide to take initiative at work, it's important to first weigh the impact of doing so against all the other alternatives available to you. While some initiatives can have tremendous impact on the organization's bottom line, others may have little or no impact on the company or your coworkers. Use the following guidelines as you decide where to concentrate your own efforts:

- **What impact does your initiative have on the organization's mission, bottom line, or strategic objectives?** Rank your initiatives based on how strongly they contribute to increasing your organization's revenues and profit. If you work for a nonprofit organization, consider which initiatives will help you most directly achieve your organization's mission in the most timely and cost-effective way. Initiatives that improve working conditions and employee morale are also important because they lead to improved financial performance.

- **Urgency does not necessarily equal importance.** Assess urgent tasks first to determine their relative importance and to see where they fit in the overall scheme of your responsibilities. Only then should you react.

- **Is your initiative someone else's responsibility?** Although you may be tempted to take initiative throughout your organization, in some cases it is best to defer your efforts to the person who is responsible for the particular product, service, or process that you wish to address. If this is the case, bring up your ideas or concerns with that person, and then let him or her take the ball and run with it.

for checking the sirens and a system for streamlining the necessary reports. After implementing the plan, the team didn't miss a deadline for the next two years, at which time an automated system was installed.

Employees on an assembly team at Monarch Marking Systems in Miamisburg, Ohio, came up with a more efficient assembly process on their own when they were faced with a deadline for assembling a two-pound bar code reader. They knew it was ridiculous to continue to assemble the product on a mechanical conveyor belt. By eliminating the conveyor belt and installing a workstation, they could face each other and simply pass around the product by hand. The employees could talk to each other and help anyone who fell behind. By the time it was over, they had reduced the square footage of their assembly area by 70 percent, cut work-in-progress inventory by $127,000, and slashed past-due shipments by 90 percent—in addition to doubling productivity.

After 80 percent of the employees in one of the departments of First National Bank of Chicago expressed dissatisfaction with their work assignments, a team of workers independently pulled together to solve the problem. After meeting together an hour a day for two months, the group recommended that the department redesign fragmented tasks into complete jobs. Manage-

A Good Team Cares for Its Members

Help each other to be right—don't look for things that are wrong.

- Look for ways to make new ideas work rather than reasons why they won't.
- If in doubt, check it out! Don't make negative assumptions.
- Help each team member win and take pride in others' victories (we, us, our—not they, them, their).
- Speak positively about each other and the organization at every opportunity.
- Maintain a positive mental attitude no matter what the circumstances.
- Act with initiative and courage, as if it all depends on you.
- Do everything with enthusiasm—it's contagious.
- Whatever you want—power, respect, enthusiasm, compassion, recognition—give it away first. What goes around comes around.

ment agreed to implement the recommendations and, as a result, employee satisfaction and performance improved dramatically.

In many organizations, the status quo of systems, procedures, processes, and reports are continued for years and years without question. In fact, the words "That's the way we've always done it" should be a warning sign to any employee who hears them. At Ameritech, a telecommunications firm based in Chicago, Illinois, an enterprising financial team, driven to cut out useless organizational red tape, submitted a

EMPOWERING TEAMS

As a member of a team, you have a choice: you can wait for someone to empower you to take action, or you can empower yourself. You have the power within yourself to be as active a participant as you want to be. It's simply a matter of taking initiative to speak up and to involve yourself in the group's discussions and activities. Here are tips for empowering yourself as a member of a team:

- Commit yourself fully to the team and to its goals.
- Take an active role in helping to define the goals of the team.
- Use your own skills to complement the skills of other members of your team.
- Take responsibility for team progress.
- Be willing to play the role of devil's advocate when necessary.

proposal to management to take action. With management's backing and armed with a huge stack of company reports, the team hit the road to visit every major Ameritech office. In face-to-face meetings, the headquarters team would hold up each report and ask the field managers, "Do you really need this report?" Some of the reports were useful, others were consolidated, and many were simply eliminated. The team discovered that one well-intentioned and hard-working employee was spending five full days a month preparing and circulating a report that nobody read! Through this team's initiative, Ameritech estimated that it eliminated the production and circulation of more than 6 million pages of reports a year.

> "Without initiative, it's impossible for a worker to grow into a leadership position."
>
> —Anonymous, from the Internet

Responding to the company's requirement to both become more productive and reduce defects, a self-managed process improvement team at ABB Industrial Systems in Columbus, Ohio, whose members had previously been involved with inspecting incoming shipments for defects, initiated a new program requiring suppliers to meet standards of excellence. The team graded each supplier on various aspects of performance. Those with poor ratings were not used again; those with high scores were invited to work with the ABB team to reduce cycle time and increase customer satisfaction. The resulting improvements in supplier performance made it possible to eliminate quality inspections of incoming materials.

> “Initiative is the fuel that feeds success. You can have two employees that are of equal cognitive abilities, but the one who takes initiative to work past established paradigms will ultimately have greater success in the workplace. As managers, we must foster staff initiative. This allows the staff member to become an entrepreneur, taking ownership of the task at hand. It works for my staff and the environment in which we work.”
>
> —STEVE DEATRICK, from the Internet

Andrea Rosen, sales and marketing manager for Living Language, an imprint of Random House Inc., in New York City, has developed a unique approach to taking initiative in meetings. Instead of waiting to be invited to participate in important company meetings, she invites herself. Says Rosen, “An important step is to be included in a variety of meetings. Even if I wasn't always included, I would ask if I could go in order to learn from higher executives. Oftentimes I believed that I could add valid points to the discussions.” And instead of being rebuffed by those holding the meetings, her interest in the workings of her organization has opened doors for her. “Doing things like that has allowed me to learn more about different departments and to grow. As a direct result of my initiatives, I was recently asked to serve on a profit-improvement committee.”

For some time, malfunctions in elevators bringing food from catering trucks to galleys in United Airlines Boeing 747 aircraft were creating a variety of problems for employees and causing flight delays for the airline. A team of concerned employees took the initiative to develop engineering blueprints and a full plan for redesigning and installing circuitry in galley elevators on its 747 jets. The new design reduced elevator malfunctions that had caused flight delays.

At General Motors, a team of innovative employees meeting at an assembly plant over a holiday break designed a shutdown-startup process for drying fans in the vehicle paint area that saved $160,000 a year in energy costs and improved paint jobs to boot.

> “All decisions should be made as low as possible in the organization. The Charge of the Light Brigade was ordered by an officer who wasn't there looking at the territory.”
>
> —Robert Townsend, Former President, Avis

In many organizations, the answer “Because we've always done it that way” is often enough to pour cold water on employee initiative or innovation. For years, auto parts manufacturer Delco-Remy paid sales taxes on items that should have been tax exempt. Certain that the company was overpaying its taxes, and realizing that there was an opportunity to save the company a substantial chunk of change, a team of accounting employees independently identified the problem and then developed solutions to it. As a result, the team saved the company $700,000 a year in taxes by identifying items exempt from sales taxes.

While some employees are content to work within the status quo, even when it's clearly broken, others are energized by the challenge of finding new ways to make old systems better. A group of people from a variety of federal, state, and local government organizations pulled together to form the Georgia Common Access Team, based in Atlanta. Through the team's initiative, the number of pages of application paperwork required to be filled out by prospective recipients of food stamps, Medicaid,

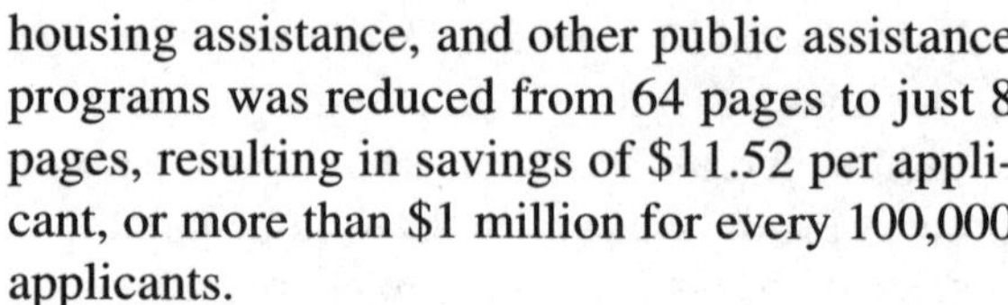

housing assistance, and other public assistance programs was reduced from 64 pages to just 8 pages, resulting in savings of $11.52 per applicant, or more than $1 million for every 100,000 applicants.

> “It took inspiration to desire the job. It took intelligence to get the job. It took political savvy to keep the job. But it takes initiative to be a part of the job!”
>
> —Lynn, from the Internet

When a management quality initiative inadvertently created production problems at Landscape Forms, Inc., a “site” furniture (benches, planters, and trash receptacles) manufacturer in Kalamazoo, Michigan, staff rose to the challenge by creating the War Room. Composed of employees from each production area and several staff members, the War Room was specifically designed to exclude the participation of managers. Says one employee, “Managers were not invited so people would feel free to say anything.” The War Room tackled the problem of late deliveries of products, reducing lead time from more than 60 days to less than 30, and dramatically improving on-time shipment performance. Some customers have actually started complaining about receiving their orders too early!

At the Tennant Company in Minneapolis, Minnesota, engineers devised a $100,000 system to streamline a particular welding operation, with the aim of stockpiling fewer finished units. When management balked at the price tag of the improvement, the team of engineers came back with a solution that cost only $25,000. Management vetoed that proposal too. Faced with an inefficient system that was costing their

company dearly in terms of wasted worker time and effort, as well as excess storage costs, a small group of welders decided to take action to solve the problem themselves. Their solution was an overhead monorail system that would carry parts from one workstation to another. To save money, the welders found some scrap I-beams in a local junkyard and bought them for less than $2,000. The new system, which the welders assembled in only two days, saved more than $29,000 in time and storage space in its first year of operation.

> “Management rewards those who take the ball and run with it. They recognize that as being intelligent and inspiring. If you don't like your job, then be intelligent and inspiring enough to do something about it. The world belongs to those who take it.”
>
> —KAREN, from the Internet

———

Bill Sanko began his intrapreneurial venture, XEL Communications, within GTE Corporation, a Stamford, Connecticut–based telecommunications giant. Sanko determined that in order for GTE to be competitive in the marketplace, the quality of products had to be improved. He pulled together a team of six coworkers and devised a plan, formed the Special Service Products Division (SSPD), and moved to Aurora, Colorado. Says Sanko, “I had the unique opportunity to start a business within a company with someone else's money. I had to take the chance to find out what I would do when confronted with creating this and being totally responsible for its success—or failure.”

———

Shop workers at Atlanta's Georgia-Pacific Corporation, the leading manufacturer and distributor of building products in the United States, created a new source of revenue by

taking the initiative to suggest that sawdust from the lumber mill be sold to nurseries as mulch.

> “To show intelligence takes initiative. To inspire others takes initiative. To use one's political savvy takes initiative.”
>
> —CAT7, from the Internet

A team of employees at the Ford Motor Company factory in Wayne, Michigan, banded together to come up with new ideas on how to reduce the annual cost of purchasing Kevlar protective gloves, used by workers who handle glass and sheet metal. The team figured out a way to wash the gloves, allowing them to be used more than once. This simple but effective idea saved Ford $115,000 a year.

TIPS FOR TEAMWORK

TAKE ACTION NOW!

1. Seek diversity in membership. The strongest teams have members from all levels of an organization, across department and division lines.

2. Select people who complement one another's skills and expertise. Enlist members who bring a perspective to the team and fill gaps in others' experience.

3. Support your teammates. "All for one and one for all" should be the credo of every team.

4. Build camaraderie. Meet offsite or get the team together for fun activities like having lunch at a restaurant or watching a movie or going to a baseball game.

5. Celebrate your successes. Achieving your goals is the reason why you started a team! Throw a party or other celebration to reinforce the efforts of those who participated in making the team successful.

Above and Beyond

We are all familiar with stories of employees who have provided customer service that is far above and beyond what is expected of a typical worker. Such stories are often memorialized within organizations, sometimes becoming the basis for formal awards such as the U.S. Office of Management and Budget's Eagle Award, or Hewlett-Packard's Golden Banana Award. They are also some of the richest examples of employee initiative that exist. Going above and beyond means you are *acting* on initiative. In customer service, you often need to act alone—and quickly. The most direct and effective way to do this is to take initiative. But going above and beyond doesn't necessarily have to be measured in terms of an extraordinary act of corporate heroism. Indeed, initiative can be defined as going outside your job description, and it can simply mean being willing to take on a bit of extra work during a particularly busy time of the year, or by being willing to take on more responsibility. And the rewards for doing so can be tangible. A recent poll of executives asked: "What do you feel is the single best way for employees to earn a promotion and/or raise?" Topping the list for 82 percent of respondents was "Ask for more work and responsibility."

Legendary Service

- Deliver more than you promise.
- Do it better than you did before.
- Imagine what would wow the other person (your boss, customer, or colleague).
- Review your job description and make a point of routinely going beyond it.

At IntroKnocks, a business-to-business greeting card company located in New York City, the holidays mean turmoil. Hundreds of customers call to order holiday cards, or to check on their orders, or to request a catalog.

> “If no one had initiative at work, the company would never grow.”
>
> —ANONYMOUS, from the Internet

On the Monday before Thanksgiving, Iveliesse Garcia came to work an hour and a half early, as usual. “I like to get the big problems out of the way before the day starts,” says the young single mother who holds the office together. On this day, she found an order in the fax machine with an unusual request. It said, “Dear Intro-Knocks, I know I should have ordered my Thanksgiving cards weeks ago, but I forgot, and my boss wants me to send them out today. He is a raging tyrant! If I don’t send them today, I am going to get fired! HELP! PLEASE!”

Garcia called the account and told her not to worry. “How many cards need to be mailed?” “About 400,” her customer replied. Garcia first had the woman e-mail a file with the 400 names and addresses. She converted them to labels with a software program. Then she did a setup for custom imprinting on a Thanksgiving card that her customer selected. Garcia printed the custom message on the 400 cards, then stamped, sealed, labeled, and actually mailed the cards before noon. When notified that everything was done, the secretary who had goofed could not believe it. “How did you get all that done by yourself?” asked the woman. Garcia simply replied, “Obviously you are not a single parent!”

Although Ukrainian immigrant Vladimir Moskalenko of San Ramon, California, was a cartographer and part-owner of a 350-employee mapping company in Kiev, Ukraine, he had to accept a job as a school custodian to make ends meet for him and his family in his

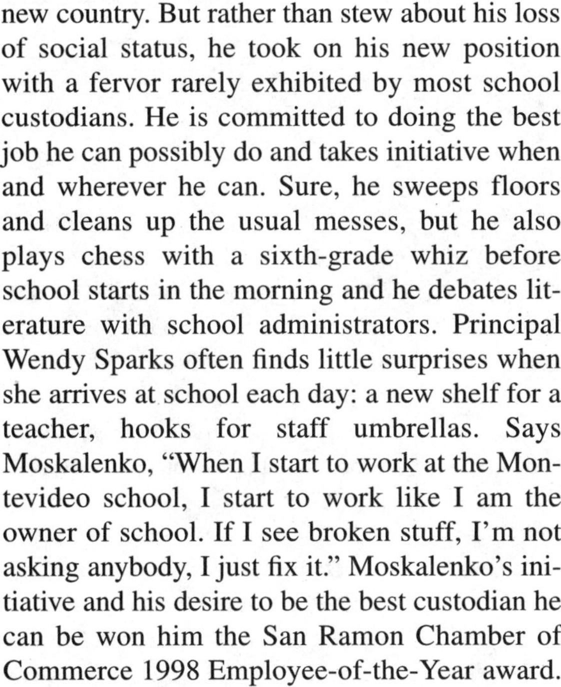

new country. But rather than stew about his loss of social status, he took on his new position with a fervor rarely exhibited by most school custodians. He is committed to doing the best job he can possibly do and takes initiative when and wherever he can. Sure, he sweeps floors and cleans up the usual messes, but he also plays chess with a sixth-grade whiz before school starts in the morning and he debates literature with school administrators. Principal Wendy Sparks often finds little surprises when she arrives at school each day: a new shelf for a teacher, hooks for staff umbrellas. Says Moskalenko, "When I start to work at the Montevideo school, I start to work like I am the owner of school. If I see broken stuff, I'm not asking anybody, I just fix it." Moskalenko's initiative and his desire to be the best custodian he can be won him the San Ramon Chamber of Commerce 1998 Employee-of-the-Year award.

> "Management isn't about doing all the work yourself or telling people everything they should do; it's about getting your team to make decisions for themselves and consider new angles."
>
> —Amanda Lathroum, Manager of Software Services, Netscape Communications Corporation

---

At the Los Banos *Enterprise* newspaper in Los Banos, California, employees receive the P.O.T.S. (for "Pulling Out The Stops") award for going above and beyond the call of duty. Winners of the esteemed trophy—a flowerpot in which a bathroom plunger is planted—include a composing department employee who drove 40 minutes back from his home to fix a computer glitch holding up newspaper production, a bilingual sales representative who took the initiative to produce a Spanish-language section in the paper once a month (which has doubled in size every month since), and two

PUTTING YOURSELF IN YOUR CUSTOMER'S SHOES

BE YOUR OWN BOSS

A key part of being able to take initiative in helping a customer is to put yourself in the customer's position. Understanding what a customer really wants or needs is essential to delivering on that need. Yet, the longer you are in a job, the more likely it is for you to lose empathy with the customer. Here are ways to keep your customer focus fresh:

Pay attention when you're the customer. We are all customers in most walks of our lives. Pay attention to how you are treated as a customer. Who gives you undivided attention and makes you feel welcome? How do you react to such treatment? When possible, ask others who provide exceptional customer service how they are able to do it. What keeps their approach to dealing with customers fresh?

Think about what would be of value if you were the customer. As you deal with customers, try to put yourself in their situation. When possible, ask customers what they think you should do to help resolve their problems. If possible, try to identify multiple solutions to increase the chances that you can meet their needs. Experiment with different potential solutions and scenarios by being proactive. As you learn a customer's problems or needs, imagine doing something that you have never done before to help them. Try to follow through and meet that need.

Have fun with the customer. Focus on enjoying your job and enjoying your interaction with customers. Vary the way you go about your job tasks whenever possible. Be in the present as you focus on and deal with others.

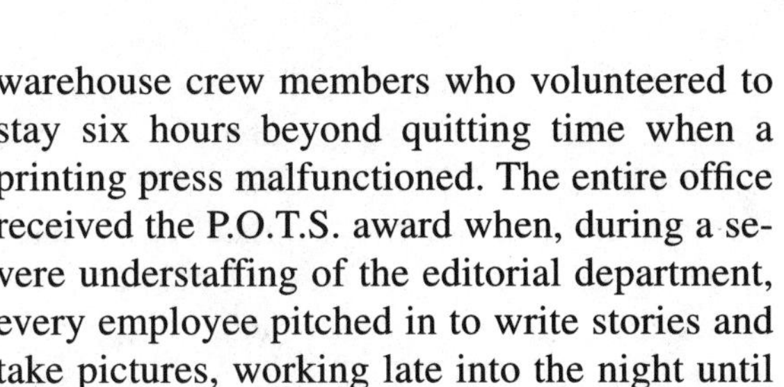

warehouse crew members who volunteered to stay six hours beyond quitting time when a printing press malfunctioned. The entire office received the P.O.T.S. award when, during a severe understaffing of the editorial department, every employee pitched in to write stories and take pictures, working late into the night until the paper was done. Says publisher Rhonda Lowe, "The exciting thing about this award is that people have won it for both small and large contributions."

> "Initiative shows several things: a willingness to work, a curiosity, a drive to improve upon what is, and an intelligence to find that better, quicker way."
>
> —Glen Mattiello, from the Internet

Despite Ileana Suchta's 16-hour days enrolling customers in Mary Kay Cosmetics' Summer '98 Preferred Customer Program, and volunteering as a corporate helper for telephone operating systems, she still found time to be a role model for 12 girls who needed guidance. On very short notice, she received a call asking Mary Kay, Inc., based in Dallas, Texas, to sponsor a group of pregnant teenage girls in a job-shadow day at Mary Kay, where they would have the opportunity to follow Mary Kay employees through a typical workday. Suchta jumped at the chance and took the initiative to personally arrange for these young women to spend half a day touring Mary Kay's office, the museum, telephone operating systems, and information systems technologies. She also arranged for the group to have lunch in Mary Kay's restaurant and to listen to Mary Kay moms talk about their jobs. And to top it off, each girl received a gift bag of Mary Kay products.

Traits of Star Initiators

According to Robert Kelley, author of *How to Be a Star at Work*, masters of star-quality initiative do the following:

- They seek out responsibility above and beyond the expected job description.
- They undertake extra efforts for the benefit of coworkers or the larger group.
- They stick tenaciously to an idea or project and follow it through to successful implementation.
- They willingly assume some personal risk in taking on new responsibilities.

Looking for a place to meet and lunch for six, Richard DeBurgh, chairman of the Child Nutrition Research Committee of the California Association of School Officials, called a colleague at the Corona Norco Unified School District in Sacramento for help. Meg Fleig quickly agreed to help DeBurgh out. The day of the meeting arrived, and when lunch was served, five custom-made deluxe salads were brought out to the delighted meeting participants. When DeBurgh told the staff that he preferred not to have a salad, the response was, "No problem. We have a special meal for you." The server disappeared into the kitchen and returned with a Taco Bell kid's meal along with three toys. It turns out that Meg Fleig had taken the initiative to find out what each attendee's preferred meal was and then prepared them without anyone on the committee knowing.

One Saturday a woman dropped by the Stew Leonard's grocery store in Norwalk, Connecticut, to order $40 worth of food to serve at lunch for 20 people. The chef at Stew Leonard's suggested that the customer buy more food than she ordered, but she decided not to. A few hours later the manager got a frantic call from the woman, wondering why the manager didn't insist that she buy more food. On his own initiative, the manager assembled another $40 worth of food and personally delivered it to the party. Not only that, but he refused payment, telling the customer, "No, it's on us." The party turned out to be for 20 real estate agents new to the

area. According to the president of Stew Leonard's, "Right after the party, all 20 came down to the store and bought hundreds and hundreds of dollars' worth of food—they all had full shopping carts."

In Orange, Connecticut, Home Depot store manager Leighton Royster received a phone call from a customer who was newly confined to a wheelchair and housebound. She was unable to maneuver her wheelchair down her front steps and wanted to know where to find a carpenter. Concerned about his customer's well-being, Royster took the initiative to donate all the materials and labor needed to construct a ramp. Not only did Royster help a neighbor, but he took advantage of the opportunity to teach store associates how to build a deck and ramp.

A complaint was received by the Pontiac Division of General Motors: "This is the second time I have written you, and I don't blame you for not answering me, because I kind of sounded crazy, but it is a fact that we have a tradition in our family of ice cream for dessert after dinner each night. But the kind of ice cream varies, so every night, after we've eaten, the whole family votes on which kind of ice cream we should have and I drive down to the store to get it. It's also a fact that I recently purchased a new Pontiac and since then my trips to the store have created a problem. You

> "Having initiative means you are a doer. It takes a doer to accomplish anything. You can have intelligence and all the best intentions and ideas in the world, but without being a doer nothing will be accomplished."
>
> —D. Benedictos, from the Internet

> "Initiative is very important. If you have initiative, then you will learn and develop the intelligence to play the political savvy game."
>
> —RHONDA, from the Internet

see, every time I buy vanilla ice cream, when I start back from the store my car won't start. If I get any other kind of ice cream, the car starts just fine. I want you to know I'm serious about this question, no matter how silly it sounds: 'What is there about a Pontiac that makes it not start when I get vanilla ice cream, and easy to start whenever I get any other kind?'"

The Pontiac GM president was understandably skeptical about the letter, but he sent an engineer to check it out anyway. A successful, obviously well-educated man who lived in a fine neighborhood greeted the GM employee. He had arranged to meet the customer just after dinnertime, so the two hopped into the car and drove to the ice cream store. It was vanilla ice cream that night and, sure enough, when they returned to the car, it wouldn't start. The engineer returned for three more nights. The first night, the man got chocolate. The car started. The second night, he got strawberry. The car started. The third night he ordered vanilla. The car failed to start.

Now the engineer, being a logical person, refused to believe that this man's car was allergic to vanilla ice cream. He arranged, therefore, to continue his visits for as long as it took to solve the problem. And toward this end he began to take notes: he jotted down all sorts of data: time of day, type of gas used, time to drive back and forth, etc.

In a short time, he had a clue: the man took less time to buy vanilla than any other flavor.

Why? The answer was in the layout of the store. Vanilla, being the most popular flavor, was in a separate case at the front of the store for quick pickup. All the other flavors were kept in the back of the store at a different counter, where it took considerably longer to find the flavor and get checked out.

Now the question for the engineer was why the car wouldn't start when it took less time. Once time became the problem, the engineer quickly came up with the answer: vapor lock. It was happening every night, but the extra time it took to get the other flavors allowed the engine to cool down sufficiently to start. When the man got vanilla, the engine was still too hot for the vapor lock to dissipate.

> "Initiative means having the imagination, intelligence, and 'energy' to get out there and get whatever needs to be done, done! Be positive!"
>
> —Anne, from the Internet

After calling a computer manufacturer and being told it would take three weeks to build and deliver two laptop computers that he absolutely had to have by noon the next day, the guy running the entire video show for the Rolling Stones' recent "Bridges to Babylon" tour frantically called computer maker Gateway in North Sioux City, South Dakota. Sales representative Duffy Conway took the call and rose to the challenge by personally shepherding the order through production and out the door for overnight delivery to New York. Not only did the Stones' tour go off without a hitch, but the grateful video manager made sure that Conway got great seats and a backstage pass for one of the stops.

> “Having the ‘know-how’ just isn’t enough. One needs to have the drive to set goals and work to achieve them.”
>
> —W.D.A., from the Internet

Herschell Gordon Lewis, chairman of Communicomp, a direct marketing division of Bozell, Jacobs, Kenyon & Eckhardt in Fort Lauderdale, Florida, tells a story about a surprising bit of initiative that his wife encountered while shopping for Starbucks coffee over the telephone. Says Lewis, “My wife has been a loyal Starbucks customer. She called to reorder a blend we’d been enjoying for months. Oops! The telemarketer said they had dropped that mix of coffee. ‘Okay,’ said Margo, ‘in that case I’m back to Gevalia [a competing brand of coffee].’” However, Margo soon found a package in her mailbox from Jan Brown, a direct-response associate at Starbucks. The letter accompanying the package said, “Although we cannot always promise to offer each of the coffees we’ve carried in the past, because of your extensive customer history we have created a special gift for you based on the coffees you have ordered.” Enclosed with the letter were two pounds of the coffee she had wanted. Jan Brown’s initiative had won back a loyal Starbucks customer.

Liloo Alim, main concierge at the Four Seasons Hotel in Toronto, Canada, spent a few hours after work every day for several months looking at condos for a guest who was moving to the area. When the guest, a businessman from Washington, finally bought a condo across the street from the hotel, he continued to use Alim to send flowers on his behalf and make restaurant reservations—free of charge. Explaining why she continues to go out of her way

to assist her former guest, Alim says, "He's always a potential client in other cities."

One fine January day—with three inches of fresh snow on the roads, and the promise of more to come—David Lubetkin, president of Industrial Edge USA, an apartment house supply company in Orange, New Jersey, got a call from a customer. Says Lubetkin, "He urgently needed 60 pounds of rock salt to be delivered to one of the properties his company manages—100 miles away in Pennsylvania." Unfortunately, all of the company's delivery trucks were already on the road making deliveries, but Lubetkin soon found a rental truck and hit the road. After a four-and-a-half-hour trek at an average speed of 20 miles per hour, Lubetkin made the delivery to a very happy customer.

> "When supervisors and coworkers see that you are willing to do what it takes to get things done, you will more than likely be recognized and compensated for it."
>
> —CB, from the Internet

When Tony Heineman, an account executive at KTUL Channel 8 in Tulsa, Oklahoma, called a client who was a media buyer at a local company, he knew something was wrong. It turned out that she was stressed about car repairs that she needed but couldn't afford to make. Heineman told her, "Don't move, I'm on my way." He picked up her car at the studio and left her his Toyota Camry. Says Heineman, "I brought her car to a friend of mine who is a mechanic and who I knew would do the job at no charge." The next day, Heineman returned the newly repaired car to his very relieved client.

How to Make a Good Impression

According to Roger Ailes, chairman and CEO of Fox News, people have only seven seconds to make a good impression. And making a good impression can make all the difference when it comes to influencing others. Here is his advice:

- **Amp up your attitude.** When meeting someone for the first time, concentrate on your energy level. If you don't demonstrate an energetic attitude on your first day, you're screwing up.
- **Recognize face value.** Many business executives believe a poker face is a strategic advantage. Sometimes it is. But often you gain credibility with an audience when they feel you're open. The viewer generally perceives the more vulnerable personality as being stronger and less afraid.
- **Give your message a mission.** Let other people blab. When you talk, have an agenda.

At Dallas, Texas–based Southwest Airlines, where pilots sometimes jump in to help at the boarding gate, and where ticket agents sometimes pitch in to load baggage, a reservations clerk took a call from a concerned customer who was getting ready to put his 88-year-old mother on a flight to St. Louis. The customer was afraid that his mother wouldn't be able to negotiate the change of planes in Tulsa. No problem, replied the clerk, "I'll fly with her as far as Tulsa and make sure she gets safely aboard the St. Louis flight."

One day a distraught guest at Walt Disney World's Polynesian Village Resort in Orlando, Florida, relayed her disappointment to the front-desk hostess about losing several undeveloped rolls of film. The clerk asked the guest to give her a couple of rolls of fresh film, and then she promised that she would take care of the rest. According to Valerie Oberle, vice president of Disney University's Guest Program, "Two weeks later, the guest received a package at home. In it were photos of the entire cast of our luau show, personally autographed by each performer. There were photos of the Disney parade and fireworks from the theme park, taken by the front-desk hostess on her own time, after work."

One day Bill Wallace, a customer service technician with Jones Intercable cable television in Independence, Missouri, answered a

service call for a customer who was confused about which channel was where on the cable system. Once Wallace realized that his customer couldn't read the channel lineup card because cataracts obscured her vision, he quickly returned to the office, enlarged the card on a copy machine, laminated it, and then personally delivered it to his excited and grateful customer.

> “Initiative means making things happen. And that's what we need!”
>
> —Yvan, from the Internet

When a guest celebrating a birthday at Italianni's restaurant in Plymouth, Minnesota, ordered a Peanut Buster Parfait for dessert—an item not on the restaurant's menu—waitress Deb Gordon rose to the occasion. Within 15 minutes, Deb's happy guest received his favorite dessert, delivered fresh from a local Dairy Queen.

When a guest at the Guest Quarters Suites Hotel in Waltham, Massachusetts, ripped a suit that the local dry cleaner couldn't repair overnight, Juan Gallego, a member of the bell staff, took the suit home with him. Gallego's mother repaired the suit and he delivered it in time for the executive to wear to a meeting the next morning. And, in the course of adopting a child, a couple made repeated visits to a Guest Quarters Suite Hotel in Philadelphia, Pennsylvania. When the new parents came to town to pick up the infant and bring her back to the hotel, they discovered that hotel employees had taken the initiative to turn their suite into a fully decorated nursery, complete with crib, balloons, a teddy bear personalized with the baby's name,

NAÏVE LISTENING

TOOL BOX

To help others, you need to start with being clear about what is helpful to the other person. The skill of clarifying exactly what the customer or other person needs is thus critical and involves listening in a new way; it is sometimes referred to as "naïve listening." Here are guidelines to encourage a person to open up so that you can understand what he or she is saying:

Don't assume you know what the other person wants. Too often in our interpersonal communications, we think we know what others want before they even have a chance to say it. This is especially true when we work in a position where we have had multiple requests of a similar nature. It becomes very easy to quickly categorize requests by how they are similar instead of more fully exploring how they are potentially different. As Stephen Covey advocates: "Seek to understand before you seek to be understood."

Encourage the other person to elaborate. Communication starts when you stop talking and asserting your opinion and instead let the other person share what he or she needs. Encourage the other person to elaborate on what is being said by asking for more information, examples, or open-ended questions. In the process you will discover the person's depth of experience, his or her logic, preferences, and much more. Through head nods and verbal cues like "uh-huh," you can get the other person to expand on what is said without committing your own opinion.

Listen closely and repeat what is said for clarity. Once you have fully drawn the other person out, you can summarize and reflect what you heard in your own words, giving the other person a chance to agree or disagree with your summarization. Then, when you are sure about what the other person needs, you can suggest helpful alternatives.

and a big greeting card signed by every member of the staff.

Larry Green, a natural foods consultant for Phoenix Rising in Pittsburg, California, recently went on a trek to purchase a birthday present for his wife. Green's wife specifically wanted a tabletop fountain from the Nature Company. Says Green, "I arrived at their Concord store and was told that they were all sold out. Sandy, the clerk who was waiting on me, asked how soon I needed it. I told her my wife's birthday was the next day. Sandy then called her central tracking office and found that there was one in San Francisco. She then called the Embarcadero location and asked them to find the model I wanted. Twenty minutes later they called to say they would ship it off to me but they could not guarantee that it would be delivered in time." It would have been easy for the employee to simply tell Green that the item was out of stock, and he would have to await the store's next shipment. But instead, she took the initiative to do whatever it took to help her customer fulfill his wishes.

Says Green, "What really blew me away was that because it was being shipped from another store, Sandy would not receive credit for the sale. Her excellent customer service made me feel extremely satisfied and grateful. I went home with another substitute present that did bring joy to my wife, and told her that the fountain would arrive on Monday or Tuesday. We were both genuinely happy to find that, thanks

> “Intelligence and inspiration are important, but if you don't have the initiative to use them, what's the point? Political savvy may win you some allies, but you need initiative to recognize the benefits of these in the first place.”
>
> —JESSIE, from the Internet

> "You've got to have an atmosphere where people can make mistakes. If we're not making mistakes we're not going anywhere."
>
> —Gordon Forward, President, Chaparral Steel

to Sandy and another nameless, faceless employee in the San Francisco store, the fountain arrived on my wife's birthday. It delivers joy each and every day."

Employees at the Crystal Gateway Marriott in Arlington, Virginia, do a lot for their guests. Staffers once located three dozen daisies for a guest in the middle of a blizzard. A clerk stood behind the check-in counter for hours in socks, after lending his shoes to a guest who had forgotten his own and had to give a speech nearby. Concierge Jean Goodson had her husband bring in a tin of Tiger Balm lotion for a particularly picky guest.

Lois Frankel, author of *Overcoming Your Strengths: 8 Reasons Why Successful People Derail and How to Get Back on Track,* tells a story about a woman she met at a Christmas party. The woman, named Mary, worked for the U.S. Postal Service as a mail carrier. During the course of the conversation Mary revealed that she had been on her route for quite a few years and knew the patrons well. She mentioned that when an elderly person is housebound due to illness she'll take time out from her route to walk the person's dog. Or, at other times, when someone can't get to the grocery store she'll pick up some basics for them. Once she noticed a dog wandering the neighborhood and she recognized that it belonged to someone on her route and returned the dog to the owner. Mary

helps to dispel the negative attitudes that many people harbor about postal employees through the initiative she shows. She says she goes out of her way because she truly cares about the people on her route.

Some of the real heroes in business are employees who, through their own initiative, bring their employers far more revenue than the wages they command. That's the case with a waitress at Ruby Tuesday restaurant in Greenville, South Carolina. Hired because the manager thought she "looked friendly and welcoming," Paula Doricchi nearly single-handedly turned the chain eatery into a neighborhood hangout. She remembers customer names, favorite dishes and drinks, children's—and sometimes dogs'—names, and even greets regular customers with a kiss on the cheek. Now the restaurant has to keep two reservation lists—one just for Paula's tables! Her manager says that she raises everyone's standards and figures she's worth some $3,000 in sales per week all by herself.

> "The exact words you use are far less important than the energy, intensity, and conviction with which you use them."
>
> —Jules Rose, Vice President, Sloan's Supermarkets

While it's perhaps not too surprising to see an employee take initiative within his or her area or department, the real heroes of an organization are the men and women who are willing to do whatever it takes, even if it means crossing organizational lines, to make sure that business emergencies are handled quickly and effectively. One night after the facility had closed for business, a janitor took a phone call at a

> “To communicate, put your thoughts in order; give them a purpose; use them to persuade, to instruct, to discover, to seduce.”
>
> —WILLIAM SAFIRE, Columnist, *The New York Times*

Domino's Pizza Distribution Company warehouse. The caller was a Domino's store owner who was frantic because he was about to run out of pepperoni. Knowing what a problem this would be for the Domino's franchisee—he would lose a lot of business—the janitor decided to take action. Although delivering pepperoni to Domino's stores was not in his job description, he found the keys to a delivery truck, loaded up a box of pepperoni, and drove the several hundred miles necessary to ensure that the store wouldn't have to close down. The result was a happy Domino's pizza operator, a lot of satisfied customers, and another story of extraordinary effort on the part of the company's newest hero.

As an employee at 1-800-FLOWERS, headquartered in Westbury, New York, Madelon S. Kuhn, now a branch trainer for Global Equipment Company in Port Washington, New York, was a jack-of-all-trades. She planned special meetings, coached employees, created and presented educational and motivational programming, wrote newsletters, answered mail, and hired and trained new employees. “Problem” orders often had a way of finding their way to her desk.

On one such occasion an order had been placed with the company to send flowers to a recipient located on Johnston Island in Honolulu, Hawaii. The internal note on the order stated the customer didn't think the company could make the delivery, but he had heard that if anyone could do it, 1-800-FLOWERS was the

one to help him. Several phone representatives had tried to locate Johnston Island on a map but had given up. It was clearly time for Kuhn to step in and take action.

Says Kuhn, "The manager for the International Department told me the order could not be delivered—they had tried to get orders there before and it was impossible to do. Well, I hate being told anything is impossible. The address included a military address, so I called my local public library and found out that Johnston Island was an Air Force base in the middle of the Pacific Ocean."

Kuhn next placed a call to a United States Air Force office in New York City and spoke with Captain Thomas Barth of the Public Relations office. Kuhn continues, "Captain Barth spent over 15 minutes researching where the base was located. Joking with him, I remarked that the base must be pretty top-secret if he couldn't find the information readily. He replied, 'That's confidential information, ma'am.' Captain Barth was able to tell me that Johnston Island was located in the Christmas Islands, and he supplied me with a phone number directly to the base. The operator at the Johnston Island base sounded like he was in a tunnel and said 'over' at the end of every statement."

For the third time in several hours, Kuhn explained who she was and that she needed to get information on how to deliver flowers to someone at the base. For the third time that day Kuhn heard a chuckle, but she got the information she needed. Johnston Island was receiving mail and supplies three days a week by plane out of Honolulu. Air Macedonia (the only airline that flew to

"When I made the pitch for a prepaid freight program, I knew that one executive was concerned with customer service; another was only interested in the dollar impact; a third was extremely conscious of our public image. In my target statement I said exactly how the program would affect those areas. I tried to hit every hot button."

—EMILY RODRIGUEZ,
Corporate Director of Transportation,
Esprit de Corp

> “Put your ego on the shelf. It helps to realize that you will not be associated by name with the new process that you help create. You may be the instigator, but it only works right if you’re able to persuade others to have as much stake in a new idea as you do.”
>
> —Dennis Colard, Corporate Logistics Manager, Hewlett-Packard Corporation

Johnston Island) informed her they could sell freight space on their plane if she could get a florist to deliver to them. The flowers had to be delivered at least one hour before departure on Monday, Wednesday, or Friday afternoon.

The next step was to find a florist who would deliver to the airport. “Most florists don’t like to make airport deliveries,” says Kuhn. “They take a lot of time and money because of traffic and parking. After speaking with several shops I was able to locate the one closest to the airport. They explained for a $20 delivery fee that they could in fact make the delivery. They also noted that a special box and agriculture stamps were needed [the flowers were leaving and then reentering U.S. air space].

“With information in hand, I called my customer and informed him that for an additional cost, the flowers could be delivered. He inquired how it was possible and I told him the whole story. My customer did not believe the initiative that my company or I had taken to fill his order. After entering the last notation on the order, I placed a printed copy on the International Department manager’s desk with a message written on top: ‘Nothing is impossible.’ ”

Stew Leonard’s, a grocery store in Norwalk, Connecticut, has long been known for its terrific customer service, but sometimes even veteran managers are surprised by the initiative that employees often show on their own. For example, one deli-counter employee started to include an extra packet of mayonnaise with every tuna-fish sandwich she made. When Stew Leonard himself suggested she stop including the extra mayo pack because of the additional cost and because he personally felt it was unnecessary, the sandwich maker, Mary Ekstrand, told him, "Sorry, Mr. Leonard, my customers want the extra mayo, so I'm packing it again." A surprised Stew Leonard quickly replied, "Bravo, Mary!"

> “While I love the idea of intrapreneurship, there are potentially severe personal consequences to playing that role or serving as a champion for others. It takes good ideas, high motivation, guts, a thick skin—a true entrepreneurial spirit.”
>
> —Ned Herrman, Former General Electric Executive

When an employee team at Matt Gunter's Kentucky Fried Chicken (KFC) restaurant in Modesto, California, learned that a pair of their loyal customers were planning to celebrate their twenty-fifth wedding anniversary at the restaurant, they decided to do something special to make the event memorable. As one employee ran across the street to the grocery store to buy candles, another employee prepared a special KFC pie. Then, as one employee did his very best impression of Elvis Presley singing "Love Me Tender," the other employees brought out the candle-covered pie and presented it to the happy couple.

When an employee at a large pharmaceutical company called 800-CEO-READ, formerly Schwartz Business Books of Milwaukee, Wisconsin, to find a particular book, Kris Carmichael, the order clerk who took the call, noticed that the book was out of print. He called the author in The Netherlands immediately,

obtained a copy of the book, and had it shipped directly to the client. The book arrived on the client's desk before anyone at the four other companies he had contacted looking for the book even called back to tell him it was out of print. The pharmaceutical company was so impressed with the initiative of 800-CEO-READ's employee that they now do all their corporate orders through the company. Says Jack Court, president of 800-CEO-READ: "Our employees are able to use their best judgment to act on their best intentions because they are encouraged and supported in doing so."

DELIVERING ABOVE AND BEYOND SERVICE

TAKE ACTION NOW!

1. Be a hero! Superb service doesn't take much more effort than lousy service; it's simply an attitude adjustment.

2. Never settle for less than the best. Your work is a direct reflection of *you*. Make it shine!

3. Search for models of great service. Look around your organization and find the people who are stars at work. Study them—learn what makes them tick. See if you can do what they do.

4. Follow through on your actions. Make sure the actions you take have the desired effect—not just when you do them, but a week, a month, or a year later.

5. Encourage others to follow your example. Your refusal to compromise your standards of quality and service will motivate others to do the same.

PART III

YOUR CAREER AND YOUR LIFE

What is the difference between workers who get ahead in their careers and those who get left behind? In a word: initiative. For example, some employees make a point of seeking out opportunities to learn new things, while others are content with the status quo. Some are quick to jump on problems and turn them into opportunities; others avoid tackling challenges. Some have ideas and a plan to implement them, which they put into action; others prefer to be told what to do. As a result, some employees advance very quickly in their career, while others seem to be stuck where they are, moving very slowly or not at all.

Today's most effective employees take charge of their lives and their careers by developing plans for learning and growing in their jobs. They decide *where* they want to go, and then they plan *how* to get there. Instead of just dreaming about their plans, they take the initiative to put them into action. By doing so, these employees unleash a very powerful force that can propel them forward in their careers and personal lives by opening up an entirely new world of options.

Ultimately, life is nothing more than one long series of choices. Each choice you make takes you closer to meeting your goals or pushes you farther away from them. You can choose to either take charge of your life or let your life and circumstances take charge of you. By taking initiative, you put yourself firmly in the driver's seat, and you can bet that you'll prosper as a result.

Taking Charge of Your Career

How many times have you dreamed of learning a new skill and applying it in your organization, or becoming an intrapreneur by starting up a new product or service within your company, or transferring to a different department, division, or country? Face it. Most of us want to get ahead in our careers and be appreciated and rewarded for our ideas, skills, and contributions. Whether you aspire to ascend the hierarchy of your current organization or move on to another, you *can* take charge of your current career—and find more rewards and satisfaction in the process. The key is taking responsibility for your own career instead of waiting for someone else to do it for you. There is an ancient Sioux proverb: *If you don't know where you're going, any path will take you there.*

A life without goals is a life without direction. It takes no effort at all to get *somewhere* in life or in business. However, to get somewhere *meaningful,* you first have to know where you want to go. Once you decide where you want to go, then you can plan on how to get there. Here's an example that shows the power of setting goals: In 1953, researchers polled the graduating class of Yale University and found that only 3 percent of the graduates made a regular practice of setting goals and putting them in writing. When the researchers returned in 1973 to see how the Yale class of '53 had fared, the 3 percent of graduates who set goals and put them in writing had amassed a fortune worth more than all the wealth of the other 97 percent of their classmates combined. The power of setting goals is undeniable.

Personal Brand Equity Evaluation

Management guru Tom Peters offers the following considerations to help you figure out where you're going in your organization by looking at where you are *right now.*

1. I am known for the following 2 to 4 items. By this time next year I will be known for 1 to 2 additional items.

2. My current project is provocative/challenging me in the following 2 to 4 ways.

3. My new learnings in the last 90 days include the following 2 to 4 items.

4. My public local/regional/national/global "visibility program" consists of the following 2 to 3 items.

5. Important new additions to my Rolodex in the last 90 days are the following 2 to 4

(continued on next page)

When Molly Buchholz joined Foote Cone & Belding in Chicago, Illinois, as an advertising account executive, she gave herself a 30-day deadline to check in with the person who hired her. In preparation for her meeting, she kept a running list of things to talk about, such as whether or not her aggressive work style was okay. She wanted to know both the good and the bad so that she could improve the way she did her job. Says Buchholz, "People who expect others to come to them spend too much time waiting around. I want to be more aggressive. I want people to know I'm here."

When the director of UNICEF's gift catalog business in New York City departed unexpectedly, Edward Mills volunteered for the post. He did the job, plus his regular job, for nine months, reviving a moribund operation by, among other things, instituting a toll-free phone number. By taking on extra tasks, Mills was able to secure pay increases that were far above average for his organization. Says Mills, "The lesson is to always look for opportunities to expand the scope of your assignments. And then make sure you let the organization know exactly what you've done for them."

Emily Rodriguez, corporate director of transportation at San Francisco's Esprit de Corp, has steadily increased her corporate responsibilities by advocating new ways of using logistics as a service and marketing tool, ranging from overseas cargo consolidations to prepaid freight programs. Says Rodriguez, "You have to have the ability to use office time to dream up things without guilt. That means thinking about new ideas in the workplace, not in the car or at home in the shower."

Many managers dream about having employees who take charge of their jobs and their careers without having their hand held every step of the way. This is especially true for secretaries and clerical employees, who often find themselves caught in high-pressure, low-paying jobs with few avenues for advancement. However, your job is really what *you* make it.

In the case of Sharon Leahy, whose primary job is to be the executive assistant to the chairman of Tri-United Companies, a Skokie, Illinois–based real estate company, this truism has been taken to its ultimate conclusion. While she started with the firm as "merely" a secretary, Leahy is now a vice president, an office manager, *and* the executive assistant to the chairman. And while many executive assistants dream about being in charge while the boss is away, Leahy really is. "When the boss is away, I am completely in charge of the entire operation," Leahy says. And what does her boss think about this situation? He loves it. Says Tri-United's owner, Moshe Menora, "Any boss is looking for somebody who is assertive to the point where he or she can command without being asked to command and assist without being asked to assist."

(continued from previous page)

names; important relationships nurtured in the last 90 days include the following 1 to 3 names.

6. My principal "résumé enhancement activity" for the next 90 days is the following 1 item.

7. My résumé is specifically/substantially different from last year's in the following 1 to 3 ways.

HOW TO IMPROVE YOUR MARKETABILITY

Every employee today needs to be on the lookout to avoid becoming obsolete. With the amount of change taking place in most organizations today, this is no easy task. At least several times a year you need to conduct a systematic evaluation of your marketability and worth in your current position. Questions you should ask yourself:

- **Are you delivering more value to your employer than you were three to six months ago?** If so, what is your evidence of this? Your answer can range from increased efficiency in how quickly you handle routine responsibilities, to suggestions and cost-saving ideas you have made, to projects you have initiated and executed successfully.

- **What have you learned in your job in the last three to six months?** Since most development occurs within your current job responsibilities, you constantly need to be looking to grow and learn: master a new work procedure, become part of a cross-functional team, or volunteer to take on new tasks in your job.

- **What do you plan to learn in the next three to six months?** Are opportunities coming up, or can you create circumstances for advancement at work? Who in your department or elsewhere in the organization should you make an effort to meet, and what could you learn from them? What external trends suggest skills and knowledge you should seek to acquire? What associations can you join? What publications can you subscribe to?

Taking time to access what qualities and abilities you have to offer as an employee is a starting point for improving your worth to yourself, your existing employer, and potential employers.

So how did Leahy position herself to take on this high level of responsibility? The extent of Leahy's education after high school was secretarial school, unlike that of her college-degreed peers in management. But Leahy took the initiative to learn everything she could about the business by questioning her boss about the mechanics and philosophy of acquisitions and other corporate decisions and by volunteering to work a schedule usually in excess of 60 hours a week.

In addition, she learned how to become an irreplaceable asset for her boss by anticipating exactly what he would need well before he had a chance to ask for it. She is active in the field, writing articles about her chosen career and even making speaking engagements. She has also mastered the art of self-promotion, mailing out articles by or about her to hundreds of friends, relatives, and business associates. However, when promoting her accomplishments to her boss, she knows where to draw the line. Says Leahy, "You can't come in each week and say, 'I did this or that,' that's childish. But when there's a big coup, I'll mention it."

When asked why many secretaries and administrative and executive assistants find themselves trapped in dead-end jobs, Leahy maintains that the problem isn't the job, it's the attitude of the person in it. "Some people stay in the corner because they're afraid to take a risk or just don't want to go beyond their scope. They just come in and put in their time and set themselves up for failure." Clearly, that

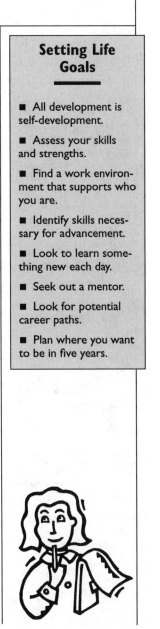

Setting Life Goals

- All development is self-development.
- Assess your skills and strengths.
- Find a work environment that supports who you are.
- Identify skills necessary for advancement.
- Look to learn something new each day.
- Seek out a mentor.
- Look for potential career paths.
- Plan where you want to be in five years.

Warning Signs of Career Change

We all sense when it's time to move on in our careers. However, some of us ignore the feelings until we find ourselves stuck in a dead-end position years later. From a recent article in the *San Francisco Examiner and Chronicle*, here are business writer Carole Kanchier's 11 deadly warning signs that you need to make changes in your career:

1. Is your body sending you messages? Do you have lingering colds? Trouble getting out of bed on a workday?

2. Are you constantly thinking, "I can hardly wait till Friday?" Do you often watch the clock?

3. Do you frequently daydream on the job?

4. Do you call in sick even when you're not?

5. Do you often arrive late for work?

6. Have your performance and productivity slipped?

(continued on next page)

has never been a problem for Sharon Leahy, and it never will be.

When Elisabeth Drumm, then an administrative staffer at Ziff-Davis Publishing, headquartered in New York City, learned that her job might be eliminated, she immediately scheduled a meeting with one of the company's human resources representatives to explore her options. Drumm let the representative know that she was a dedicated employee and that she would like to be considered for a job as a sales associate—a step up—if her job were to be eliminated. She got the job and was able to stay with Ziff-Davis. Says Drumm, "If you want to stay in the same company, you've got to put effort into staying. I had an inner knowing about what to do and a strong desire to move to a new place and start a new job."

Psychologist Sy Friedlander discovered long ago that having only one job just didn't provide him with the satisfaction that was necessary in his life. As a result, he has woven a career tapestry of several part-time jobs that interrelate, maximize his skills and abilities, and provide expression for his passion. His job titles have included director of quality assurance for a social service agency, consultant to a school system, and teacher. Says Friedlander, "I have mobility in my career because I know what I do best and am learning how to apply it to marketplace needs. Rather than trying to fit myself

into a job opening, I have learned to first assess what I have and *want* to contribute. Then I evaluate how my skills and desires add value in the marketplace."

Everyone knows that the Internet has been a boon to companies, which have a new and efficient way to reach millions of potential customers. However, many people are just now learning that the Internet can be a tremendous tool for uncovering salary data that can be used to great advantage when negotiating starting pay rates with new employers. Like many other job seekers, Holly Peckham, an account executive at Schwartz Communications in Waltham, Massachusetts, wanted to know how much pay she should expect to get to start in her next job.

Peckham devoted herself to finding sources for salary data and discovered what she was looking for on the Internet, at a web site created by Marshall Consultants, a New York executive-search firm. She found summaries of salary data for more than 16,000 communications professionals. Bingo. After wading through the data, Peckham realized that, based on her experience in the field, she should be making about $37,000 a year, $9,000 more than what she was making as an assistant account executive at Schwartz Communications. When Peckham received a job offer of $32,000, she declined it. "I told them the national average was between $36,000 and $38,000 and that I would be happy to come for between $34,000 and $36,000. My hands were shaking." She eventually accepted

(continued from previous page)

7. Do you have many disagreements with colleagues or superiors?

8. Do you feel withdrawn at work?

9. Does the prospect of spending a whole day at work get you down?

10. Will remaining with the organization for the remainder of your working life enable you to achieve your career dreams?

11. Is your work damaging your confidence? Your health? Your personal and family life? Other life facets?

According to Kanchier, giving two or more yes answers suggests that you are dissatisfied with your job, and it is time to take action.

NETWORKING MADE EASY

One of the most important skills you can develop to enhance your career is networking, that is, taking time to connect with others who share your professional interests. Here are field-tested ways to connect with others:

■ **Call individuals doing work you admire.** Most people are willing to speak to another person who shows an interest in their work, job, or opinions. Often called "informational interviewing," this tactic is not reserved simply for job hunting, but can be a viable way for you to develop lasting professional contacts. Be sure to ask for referrals of other individuals the interviewer recommends you contact.

■ **Develop your contact list**. At the end of the day, think about who you met at work, lunch, or after work and list them in your database with information about what they do, their interests, and so on. Plan a follow-up breakfast or lunch with someone you've met to get to know them better. By developing your contacts, they will be there when you need them.

■ **Join professional associations.** It's easy to compile an excellent source of professional contacts in your community by joining professional associations that interest you. Such groups typically host monthly meetings and annual conferences that allow you to develop an even broader array of contacts.

■ **Write articles for trade and industry journals.** Not only will you feel good to see your work in print, but you'll dramatically raise your profile—both inside and outside your organization.

■ **Don't be afraid to use your professional network to seek referrals and additional contacts.** In fact, calling on others will tend to strengthen relationships and increase the likelihood that they will call on you for help as well.

$34,000—a 21 percent increase over her previous salary.

Like an archaeologist digging for the evidence of some lost civilization, Charles Wetzel, a 1998 graduate of Southern Methodist University in Dallas, Texas, discovered an innovative way to determine how much money he should make in his first job. Using the power of the Internet, Wetzel reviewed the pay rates posted by companies looking to fill job vacancies—either through company sites or through dedicated help-wanted sites. After much research, he came up with a number that he felt reflected what he was worth in the job marketplace. When Wetzel received an offer of employment from a transportation company in New Jersey that came in just over $30,000 a year, he turned it down. Wetzel says, "In my eyes, they fell $10,000 short." Instead, he accepted an offer as a management consultant with Ernst & Young LLP—with a starting salary of more than $40,000. With the typical 1998 college graduate earning about $30,000, Wetzel is very proud of his newfound paycheck. "I beat [that average] by over ten grand. I didn't sell myself cheap."

> "Initiative is an attribute to be sought after. The person who can think ahead and do what he or she sees needs to be done is an asset to the employer, saving him or her time, stress, and probably money."
>
> —Anonymous, from the Internet

Robert L. Fulford, purchasing manager for Varian Ion Implant Systems in Gloucester, Massachusetts, decided on his own to go beyond his job responsibilities and take an active role in the development of the New England

> “In the past, career management meant, Get the org chart and plot a line as far up as possible. That's not the name of the game anymore. You need to figure out what skills will be relevant in the future and to map out projects to develop those skills.”
>
> —John Kotter, *The New Rules: Eight Business Breakthroughs to Career Success in the 21st Century*

Suppliers Institute, a consortium of large private and public businesses and state and federal agencies dedicated to helping small businesses produce and deliver higher-quality goods more effectively and efficiently. As a result, a large number of companies, including Fulford's Varian Ion Implant Systems, save money and receive their needed supplies more quickly. By taking the lead on such initiatives, Varian employees gain a tremendous sense of accomplishment and pride. Says Fulford, “It's as though I don't have a boss; I'm my own boss. I take full responsibility, consistently, for managing the purchasing process.”

Sometimes, initiative can come from unexpected places. Executive recruiter Korn/Ferry International joined with the *Wall Street Journal* to create an electronic job-search venture called Futurestep. One popular feature of Futurestep is a free analysis of a client's salary and bonus potential. However, much to Korn/Ferry's surprise, a group of the company's recruiters ran a salary and bonus analysis on themselves and discovered that they were underpaid—to the tune of 18 percent below prevailing rates. Korn/Ferry recruiter Peter Reed says that Futurestep will be a “part of my action plan come review time” next spring. As a direct result of his initiative in pushing the salary issue, Korn/Ferry increased Reed's base salary 10 percent, to about $80,000 a year. Remarks Korn/Ferry chief operating officer Windle Priem, “I'm sure we could have people in certain

markets where, relative to a competitor, we might be under market." With Futurestep, he says, "we're certainly creating challenges for ourselves."

When his application to Williams College was rejected in 1989, Bo Peabody, founder of Tripod, an Internet community headquartered in Williamstown, Massachusetts, didn't just crumple up his rejection letter and slink off to his second-choice college. Says Peabody, "I called the admissions office and told them, 'I reject your rejection. I'm coming there anyway.'" A year later he did.

For years, Marcia Felth, senior consultant and business program manager for Digital Equipment Corporation, headquartered in Maynard, Massachusetts, struggled to balance the expectations of her bosses and her colleagues with her growing family. When Digital began a layoff of workers a few years ago, Felth asked to be laid off. According to Felth, "My boss responded, 'You're a top performer; I can't lay you off. What else can I do for you?'" That something else meant creating a new, 20-hour-a-week job for Felth to conduct workforce planning for the company's information technology group. By taking charge of her career, Marcia Felth got the best of both worlds—a career *and* a life.

Be in Control

Take charge of your work life now by:

- Deciding what your real-life goals are
- Considering all the options available to you
- Preparing a plan to achieve your goals
- Working with your supervisor to make your plan a reality
- Periodically reviewing your progress and making adjustments as necessary

HOW TO ASK FOR A RAISE

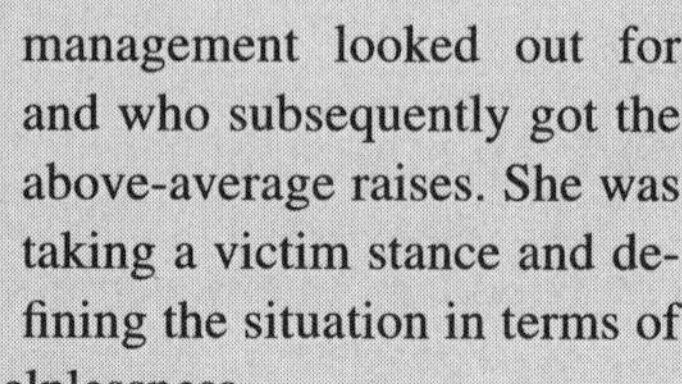

When it comes to getting raises, employees often expect their manager to look out for them if they've worked hard and are doing a good job. However, when they get the standard increase for their organization for the year—say 4 or 5 percent—they are often frustrated, not knowing what they could have done to have received a larger raise. The secret to getting an above-average raise (provided you're an above-average performer) is making the case for your raise from your manager's perspective. Putting yourself in your manager's shoes for a moment can help you make his or her job easier in justifying your increase.

Consider the story of a woman who was flying to Denver to meet her manager for her annual performance review. During the flight, she lamented to a neighboring passenger how raises in her organization tended to be doled out as part of a good-old-boy network, and that the up-and-comers were the ones who management looked out for and who subsequently got the above-average raises. She was taking a victim stance and defining the situation in terms of her helplessness.

Her time would have been better spent making the case for why she deserved an increase based on (1) work she's done, (2) her dependability (turnover was an issue in this organization), and (3) whether she helped her manager reach his or her goals. The woman's neighbor suggested that she state her salary expectation, why it needed to be more than she received in past years, and that with the suggested pay increase, she could be counted on for another year of dependable performance to the organization and the manager. The tip worked like a charm and she received a record pay increase.

The following suggestions will help prepare you to ask for a raise:

■ **Determine the market worth for your job.** Your salary will typically reflect the going rate for positions with similar responsibilities in your geographic area. Try to determine your market worth for your responsibilities (look beyond your current job title). Do you have special expertise, knowledge, or skills? Do you act autonomously, with little if any direction? Do you provide direction to others, even if they do not directly report to you? Do you have authority to make decisions, spend money, or use company resources? Do you represent your manager or the company to others? These factors indicate the level of your position and your subsequent worth within the organization.

- **Show how you have added value to the organization.** If you can show that your activities have led to increased revenues for the organization, then it is logical to suggest that you should share in those revenues. What projects and responsibilities have you taken on since your last salary review? How have those activities led directly or indirectly to increased revenues for the organization? Where have you taken initiative to do more than was asked of you? Have you exceeded expectations (and results) for your manager? Be specific. How have you personally helped your manager look good?

- **State what you expect for an increase and why that amount is justified.** Based on your diligence, you should be able to identify—and support—a specific increase. If you do your homework and are proactive in stating what you expect, you make it easier for your manager to agree and, if necessary, fight for your request with others in the organization. If your assessment is accurate, you will have given your manager a case to champion! Be sure to state what this salary increase will do for your ongoing commitment to your job, the manager, and the organization.

You can foster a positive outcome by setting up expectations before a performance period to minimize the degree of subjectivity your manager might have about your performance. Doing this allows you to take action to minimize reaction and the potential of negative surprises in the workplace.

> "The key to success is to get out into the store and listen to what the associates have to say. It's terribly important for everyone to get involved. Our best ideas come from clerks and stockboys."
>
> —SAM WALTON, Founder, Wal-Mart

Although Deborah F. Mulloy liked her full-time job as nurse manager for University Hospital in Denver, Colorado, she wanted more time to devote to her family, to teach nursing, and to consult for private industry. Mulloy decided that job sharing might be the best option for her. After conducting a literature search on the topic of job sharing, and gathering ample evidence that her hospital could greatly benefit from such a change, she presented her plan to management. It was accepted, and now Mulloy works a 16-hour workweek, while her job-sharing partner Joanne works a 24-hour workweek. Says Mulloy, "Joanne and I are both determined to make this work, so we tape-record messages to each other every day. We also reviewed our job description so that our responsibilities were clearly defined and all objectives could be met."

Putting your job on the line can be the ultimate form of initiative. When Donna Dubrinsky of Apple Computer in Cupertino, California, got tired of having to defend her department's distribution strategy to the rest of the company, she took charge of her career by threatening to resign if her boss's boss didn't allow her to make changes without the interference of a task force. His boss, and then-company president John Sculley, agreed.

While working at Wang Laboratories in Billerica, Massachusetts, Patricia Stimpson,

a software development engineer, longed to find more significance in her life. Says Stimpson, "Life had to have a deeper purpose than my job and raising children. I was feeling a hollowness; part of myself was not feeling fully developed. I was using my brain; I was a new mother; but part of me was not being enriched." In response, Stimpson began to explore her spiritual values—love, peace, oneness, collaboration rather than competition. As a result, while still working full time for Wang, she started a successful new business named Abundance, which taught adults about spiritual living.

> "The way for a young man to rise is to improve himself every way he can, never suspecting that anybody wishes to hinder him."
>
> —Abraham Lincoln

Joanne Griffin, now corporate vice president of administration for Enterprise Rent-A-Car, tells how taking initiative when she worked for Xerox Corporation had a huge impact on her career. "My biggest professional turning point came to me in the most mundane possible form. It was a job posting, a blue sheet tacked to a bulletin board. The posting was for a 'sales/system user liaison.' Who knew what that meant? The man I saw about the job barely seemed to know himself. But all I could see was opportunity. I was offered the job, and I took it."

It took Griffin a couple of weeks to figure out what her goals were: to create a computer system to be used by field personnel for tracking accounts. She rode with sales reps to determine what they needed and put together a team of software people. Griffin and her team created Xerox's first computerized system for its sales force.

Good Advice

John Challenger, president of Challenger Gray & Christmas, a Chicago outplacement firm, offers this advice to those who want to take initiative and get ahead at work: "Sweep up projects that are not being done by anyone else."

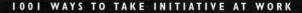

"The new system worked like a charm. The sales force now had access to better data and could access it four times faster than they'd been able to in the past; forecasts and what-ifs also were feasible for the first time. [In fact, the system, with upgrades, is still in use today.] A project no one wanted ended up earning me two promotions. Soon, I received the ultimate in plum jobs: I was allowed to create my own projects."

For some time, Paul H. P. Christen, an employee at Addison-Wesley Publishing Company in Reading, Massachusetts, had noticed that the company's LAN (Local Area Network) was a key ingredient in the way employees communicated internally and externally with customers and service providers. As a result, Christen resolved to land the job as LAN support specialist within his company. "Essentially, I volunteered my expertise to make the LAN system more accessible to users by, for example, writing a training manual and resource guide and giving seminars on its use. As I took on these responsibilities, I checked in with my boss to let him know what I was doing. I also asked him, 'Where do you see this project going in the future?' His answers helped me to sort through my own questions: 'Will *I* be able to carry this project into the future?'" The answer to this last question was yes, and Christen got the job he wanted by *doing* it.

After watching the fitness training and exercise company he worked for begin to fail, instructor Patrick Avon undertook the ultimate employee initiative by buying the company and turning it into a military-style boot camp for businesspeople in the Washington, D.C. area. His company, Sergeant's Program, has grown from an initial enrollment of four individuals to 600 avid participants who train in 15 different locations in the D.C. metro area; it grosses more than $1 million a year.

When the marketing department at her financial institution changed, and her job was suddenly put at risk, Lisbeth Wiley Chapman decided to take action. Anticipating the coming layoffs, Chapman began a five-month search for a new career. As a result, Chapman started her own company—Ink&Air—a niche public relations firm in Norwood, Massachusetts. Says Chapman, "The fear of starting a company was far worse than the reality of getting it done."

As vice president for marketing at Addison-Wesley Publishing Company in Reading, Massachusetts, Joyce Copeland realized that her fast-track career was causing her to miss out on the rest of her life. Says Copeland, "I had a terrific job, was earning plenty of money, but had no life. I was exhausted all the time." Copeland traded her high-power job for a new position as writer-editor for Boston-based

> "Be entrepreneurial. What one needs in government, as in the private sector, is imagination. If you can come up with something a little different in the way of understanding a problem, or approaching it in a way that combines different resources, then . . . you won't have to wait for opportunities; you'll make your own."
>
> —Alan Keyes, Former U.S. Assistant Secretary of State

> “Three people were at work on a construction site. All were doing the same job, but when each was asked what his job was, the answers varied. ‘Breaking rocks,’ the first replied. ‘Earning my living,’ the second said. ‘Helping to build a cathedral,’ said the third.”
>
> —Peter Schultz, CEO, Porsche

consulting firm Work/Family Directions, Inc. Now she commutes to her job a couple of times a week and works from her home office the rest of the week—at the times she chooses. Says Copeland, “The change I’ve made has given me the chance to explore and live life fully.”

On a summer job 20 years ago, Bob Freese figured out a way to do his job and the jobs of two other employees at the same time. Unfortunately, Freese’s supervisor was not as excited about this discovery as he was. Says Freese, “The supervisor told me never to bring ideas like that to him and to do the job the way he showed me. I knew from that point on that if I ever had a company of my own, I would ask for employee input.” And he did. Today, Freese heads Alphatronix in Research Triangle Park, North Carolina, one of the best employers in the United States according to *Inc.* magazine, and he has the opportunity to put his words into action every day of the week.

Hewlett-Packard’s Michael Cyr has found that he can take charge of his job and his work life by proactively choosing projects that have the highest visibility with management. For example, one of his current projects involves designing measurement systems to track Hewlett-Packard’s safety performance. The project isn’t glamorous, but it has a high profile. Cyr decided to work on safety after a senior company executive gave a speech about its

importance to the company. "I choose projects I get excited about," Cyr says. "It's an emotional response. And part of what excites me is knowing that a project matters. When top management recognizes what you're working on, you get validation and support."

Jane Lump, an employee at Strategic Innovations in Valparaiso, Indiana, has found that self-leadership is a terrific way to ensure that she meets the goals she has set for her personal learning and growth. Says Lump, "I am forming an informal board of directors to share ideas, encourage professional development, and act as a place to make commitments and review progress. In addition to being a source of industry information, backup for overflow work, and a group for referrals, this forum will provide quarterly planning time to share specific goals for personal learning and growth—as well as a source of encouragement and/or guilt for progress toward those goals!"

Instead of watching their struggling textile firm die a slow death at the hands of its competitors—putting their jobs and careers at risk—employees at Andover Apparel, Inc., in Dawson, Georgia, took the initiative to buy the company and then to implement a number of austerity measures to make it more competitive, including taking voluntary pay and benefit cuts (said one employee, "Benefits aren't everything—a job with lower benefits is better than

> "I want to be able to use my brain in my job and not be just a clone of my boss. Where I work, we all have to use initiative to keep the company going. I like that it makes me feel as though I am needed by MY company and that the work I do is valuable."
>
> —Fiona Gunasekara, from the Internet

> “Initiative, in my opinion, is the single most important quality one can have! In my firm, the majority of my colleagues are Ph.D. holders. Most of them are extremely intelligent but are passed over for promotion because they are unmotivated and lazy. Those promoted are those who are able to initiate, motivate, and lead the team.”
>
> —MELONY N., from the Internet

no job at all”), supplying their own toilet paper and hand towels, and even eliminating the hired janitor and doing all plant cleanup themselves. Against the odds, these actions have helped the employees save their jobs and preserve their livelihoods.

While many of the top professionals at Bell Labs have Harvard M.B.A.'s or are MIT Ph.D.'s, one employee without any college degrees, who began as an hourly line repairman, quickly caught the attention of management because of his initiative on the job. Instead of going for the quick fix when confronted with a problem, this employee looked for the cause of the problem for which he could then develop a global solution. Soon, Bell's field engineers began to call on him to troubleshoot their most troublesome system problems, and he was quickly promoted up the ranks. Today he is in charge of teams chock-full of professionals with the advanced degrees he doesn't have.

Taking initiative in your career often means deciding what your long-term job goals are, assessing what skills you possess—and lack—for reaching those goals, and then taking action to obtain any missing skills. Although Joseph Wilson first worked at J.P. Morgan as an intern while pursuing his MBA at the Johnson School of Management at Cornell University, he knew that he wanted to work in the firm's investment banking group. The bad news was that

competition for the limited number of positions in the investment banking group was *extremely* high, with the group accepting only 2 out of 30 applicants. So while Wilson was passed over by the investment banking group, he *was* picked by J.P. Morgan's commercial banking group. Says Wilson, "Partly due to my background [in accounting], I was more appealing to the commercial banking side."

> "Follow your bliss, and what looks like walls will turn into doors."
>
> —Joseph Campbell, *The Power of Myth*

And while he did quite well in commercial banking—eventually rising to the level of vice president—deep down inside Wilson knew that something was missing. What was missing was his dream of working in investment banking. "I woke up one day four years ago and realized I had to make a move," says Wilson. "But that would mean getting tangible skills I didn't have and convincing my managers that I could do it." At that very moment, Wilson resolved to do whatever it would take to reach his long-term career goals—and to live his dreams.

His first move was to the global credit group, a place where Wilson felt he would be able to develop the kinds of skills that he was weak in. His next step was to become a chartered financial analyst—the certification needed to become a portfolio manager. This was clearly a move in the right direction. According to Wilson, "It brought me up to speed on the language of the securities business and gave me a real feel for that business."

With these additional skills under his belt, Wilson got the word out that he was ready, willing, and able to accept a position in the investment banking group. He recalls, "I basically

> “People with initiative show commitment, motivation to do things, and disposition to try.”
>
> —Anonymous, from the Internet

went for broke. I wanted to make a move and to hell with caution. I was going to make my move either here or somewhere else. I was being discreet—I didn't ruffle any feathers or take inappropriate steps in my approach to this—but other managers were checking back with my managers, unbeknownst to me. Had I been more junior, this very well could have backfired. I've seen junior people get slammed for that." Wilson was offered several positions that paid more than he was making, but he had yet to get an offer from the investment banking group. Although flattered by these offers, he turned them all down. Why? Because, according to Wilson, "they weren't getting me any closer to what I wanted."

Finally, with the concerted effort of the head of Morgan's global credit group, Joseph MacHale, Wilson reached his goal—landing a position in secondary loan sales and trading. But while Wilson was happy to achieve his long-term goal, he wasn't ready to rest on his laurels just yet—he has a few more goals to accomplish before he even considers that particular option. Says Wilson, "Over the next five years, I'd like to become an extremely good salesperson. Long term, I'd like to position myself to be a portfolio manager."

Joseph Wilson is a big believer in taking initiative in his career. In fact, he sees no other option. He says, "There is no institution, given what's been happening over the last couple of years, where I would be comfortable leaving my career options in the hands of management. That's extremely dangerous, just as it is to sit

pretty with your current skills set." And would Wilson risk it all again in pursuit of the career of his dreams? "Absolutely," he says. "I expect I'll have to."

Stepping back for a moment and taking a look at the big picture of your career can pay off in many ways. After taking a course in career management, Fiona Eason, personnel manager for Knoll Pharmaceuticals, came back to her job with a much clearer idea of the role she wanted to play in the company. According to her supervisor, "The change was marked. She went from being rather stressed and uncertain about her future to taking control of the situation and overcoming the anxiety completely."

Because of this newfound clarity, her boss decided to consider her for a strategic position within the firm. He continues, "She was realistic about her strengths and that made it much easier for me to suggest that we try it." And Eason is discovering new challenges that she hadn't even imagined before she accepted her new position. While these challenges can at times be a bit unnerving, in the long run, they make for a much more satisfying job. "Sometimes I feel like a fish out of water," she says. "You're shifting so much from your familiar box of tricks, and that can be difficult individually." With the support of her boss, her coworkers, and her organization, there is no doubt that she will be able to meet this challenge head-on.

> "You can have intelligence but yet be very lazy. You may be inspired to do something, but it doesn't mean you're going to go out and do it. The only way to make it in life is to get up, get out, and do it."
>
> —Susana Bernacchi, from the Internet

The Intrapreneur's Ten Commandments

Gifford Pinchot, author of *Intrapreneuring*, offers the following tips to intrapreneurs:

1. Come to work each day willing to be fired.

2. Ask for forgiveness rather than for permission.

3. Do any task to make your dream work, regardless of your job description.

4. Follow your intuition about people and build a team of the best.

5. Work underground—publicity triggers the corporate immune system.

6. Be true to your goals, but be realistic about how to achieve them.

7. Ask for advice before you ask for resources.

8. Never bet on a race unless you are running in it.

(continued on next page)

Kathy Knight, president and CEO of Baiglobal, a market research firm in Tarrytown, New York, believes that individual initiative is an important element in getting ahead at work. According to Knight, the quality of your work is what gets you ahead, not playing games. "So many people think success is show biz and who you sit next to at the company dinner. Talent becomes visible by accomplishing things." To illustrate her point, Knight mentions the story of executive vice president Bob Skolnick. Skolnick, founder and head of Baiglobal's Competitive Tracking Services division, climbed up the corporate ladder when he developed an innovative new product—a credit-card tracking system called Mail Monitor—and built its sales from nothing into something. As a result of his work on the product, he gained recognition as an expert throughout the industry. Says Skolnick, "It allowed me to develop expertise and gain credibility in the industry," So Skolnick's initiative first led to the development of a successful new product, which led to recognition outside of the company, and eventually brought him promotional opportunities within Baiglobal.

Taking initiative made all the difference in the world for Cynthia Schmae, now a producer for the Career Channel at New York City's iVillage virtual community. Her first job out of college was working on the California senate campaign of Dianne Feinstein. When Feinstein won the election, Schmae moved to Washington, D.C., from California, asked her

former boss at the campaign office to put in a good word for her, and finagled an interview with the woman who was doing the hiring for Feinstein's Washington staff. With thousands of résumés in front of her, the interviewer offered Schmae a position in the mailroom opening mail. According to Schmae, "I put my ego on the shelf, took the job, got my foot in the door, and was promoted two months later to a position managing the mailroom staff. Several months after that I became a legislative correspondent, then a legislative analyst, and finally deputy director of special projects. The way I moved up was pure initiative. I packed up and moved across the country with no job lined up. I got there first, which is how I got a job so quickly. And once there, I offered to help everyone do anything—and I stayed late every night helping different employees with whatever they had on their plate."

(continued from previous page)

9. Keep the best interests of the company and its customers in mind, especially when you have to bend the rules or circumvent the bureaucracy.

10. Honor and educate your sponsors.

Taking initiative can lead to opportunities for employees to become *intrapreneurs,* starting entirely new lines of business and revenue sources within an already established organization. At a high-quality specialty steel manufacturer in Sweden, nonstandard lengths of steel bar were recycled as scrap. However, a young employee named Lennart in the information-processing department had an idea of how to better utilize this material. He presented his idea of using the scrap steel bars as the basis for premium-price weight-lifting equipment. Management agreed with his proposal and offered

> “Initiative is tied to attitude. Attitude, not aptitude, determines altitude. Intelligence without initiative or desire is quite stagnant.”
>
> —MARIE, from the Internet

Lennart the opportunity to develop a business line using the company's name, knowledge of steelmaking, underused capacity, and worldwide distribution network. Lennart developed the concept of the Rolls-Royce of weight-lifting gear, supported by a line of bodybuilding equipment marketed directly to athletic clubs and training institutes. He engaged some world-class weight lifters and bodybuilders to promote his equipment, and using the company's worldwide marketing and distribution network, he built an export business in 22 countries. Within 12 months, Lennart had 15 employees, an impressive list of clients, and sizable sales volume. Today his equipment is approved and used in championship events all over the world.

For Microsoft's Adam Rauch, taking charge of his career meant stopping whatever he was doing for a moment and taking the time to decide the best direction to take next. Originally joining Microsoft as the first program manager for Visual Basic, he attracted Bill Gates's attention and quickly became a rising star within the company. However, when it was time for a revision to the program, Rauch decided to jump to a new project within the company. Says Rauch, “Visual Basic had created an industry. I like being able to say, ‘I was there at the beginning.’ Then I asked myself, Can I do it again? Was I just along for the ride, or was I instrumental in creating it? I wanted a new challenge.”

One day, Gates gave a speech on the rise of the Internet and Microsoft's commitment to it.

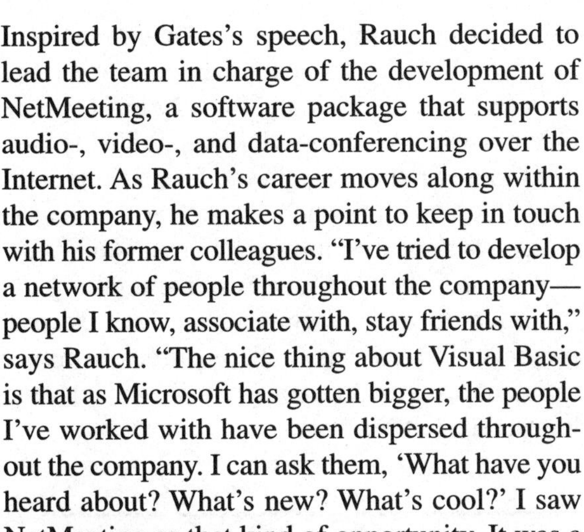

Inspired by Gates's speech, Rauch decided to lead the team in charge of the development of NetMeeting, a software package that supports audio-, video-, and data-conferencing over the Internet. As Rauch's career moves along within the company, he makes a point to keep in touch with his former colleagues. "I've tried to develop a network of people throughout the company—people I know, associate with, stay friends with," says Rauch. "The nice thing about Visual Basic is that as Microsoft has gotten bigger, the people I've worked with have been dispersed throughout the company. I can ask them, 'What have you heard about? What's new? What's cool?' I saw NetMeeting as that kind of opportunity. It was a brand-new thing, a blank slate."

For Glen Larsen, senior design engineer at Bayer Corporation, a plastics manufacturer in Akron, Ohio, taking initiative isn't just something to talk about doing—it's a way of life. When Larsen and a coworker noticed that some customers were having a difficult time designing snap-fit fasteners, he decided to take action. "So we developed software that answers customers' simple questions about snap fits and helps them start designing the plastic fasteners. That way, we can be more of a resource to develop better designs rather than spending our time answering their simple questions."

But according to Larsen, there's more to success at work than simply taking initiative. You have to keep on top of the latest developments in your products and markets. He says,

Nonprofit Advice

Nonprofit organizations can benefit from the efforts of intrapreneurs just as much as for-profit organizations. Here are tips for budding intrapreneurs working in the nonprofit sector:

- Network with peers in for-profit organizations and partner with them on specific projects.
- Learn how to maximize the impact of every dollar spent on social programs.
- Become conversant in the financial terminology of the for-profit world—concepts such as sales, profit, expense, and so on.
- Participate in trade shows to promote nonprofit products and services.
- Involve members of the community in generating ideas for new products, services, and delivery systems.

> “Initiative is one of the most important things to hold on to when you want to move up in any business.”
>
> —ANONYMOUS, from the Internet

“To be effective today, you need a long-term vision of how your company can continue to be competitive and efficient. Not only must you be able to solve problems quickly and reliably, you need to retain that edge in the future. Engineers should spend time each week learning something new or how to improve a process they currently use.” By keeping current and taking the initiative to step forward and lead several projects, Larsen has both ensured customer satisfaction with the company’s products and boosted its bottom line.

PLANNING FOR ADVANCEMENT

TAKE ACTION NOW!

1. Know where you want to go. Decide where you want to be in five years, and what you want to be doing. Develop a plan for getting there.

2. Take responsibility for your own future. Don’t leave your career in someone else’s hands—it’s your life, and you should live it according to your goals and expectations, not someone else’s.

3. Build a network of contacts. A network of associates both inside and outside your organization is an invaluable asset when charting your career and making career moves.

4. Volunteer for positions of more responsibility. Managers love employees who are willing to step up to the plate and take more responsibility. As you seek more responsibility and authority, you’ll get it.

5. Seek new opportunities and challenges. The worst punishment at work is to be bored with what you do. Constantly seek out new opportunities and challenges as you complete old ones.

Learning and Education

In a recent survey, 84 percent of respondents indicated that more positions require crossover skills, especially technology-related ones. Companies that encourage employee-training initiatives often reap a huge return in increased productivity. For example, high-tech manufacturer Motorola estimates that it earns $30 for every $1 invested in employee training. However, while some organizations are very good about ensuring that their employees receive exactly the kinds and amounts of training that they need as they work their way up the ladder of success, other organizations do little or nothing to help employees manage their training needs. In this case, it's critically important that employees themselves take charge of their own learning and education programs. By taking initiative—either through employer-sponsored training programs or, if necessary, on your own—you can ensure that you get exactly the training you need. Not only that, but it's very likely that the training you receive through work will improve your life not only on the job but off the job as well.

Alvin Perelman, a pediatric endocrinologist at Phoenix Children's Hospital in Arizona, decided that continuing his education was the best way to keep up with the changing world of work. However, because the field of medicine is quickly becoming more business oriented, Perelman is studying for an M.B.A. Says Perelman, "Everything in medicine is being looked

Life-Long Learning

In his book *Eleven Lessons in Self-Leadership,* Larry Holman, founder and chairman of WYNCOM, Inc., of Lexington, Kentucky, offers these tips for building mental effectiveness—both on and off the job:

1. Increase your vocabulary by learning at least one new word daily.

2. Attend professional-development programs.

3. Turn your car into a "rolling university" by listening to motivational and educational tapes on your way to and from work.

4. Make lists of ideas for personal growth. Review them regularly to check your progress.

5. Take behavioral assessment tests to determine your strengths and weaknesses.

6. Join professional or trade associations and become an active member.

7. Contribute volunteer time to community

(continued on next page)

at now as a business, so if you're not in tune with that, you're a potential liability and may not be around." And will taking this initiative to better himself pay off? Perelman believes it will. "With an M.B.A., I can be a better liaison for the doctors with the business side of the hospital, and it will give me another skill in case my job description is not as necessary as it is now."

Editorial evangelist Brian C. Hooper of San Francisco, California, doesn't leave learning on the job to chance; he is organized and methodical in his approach. "My plan for continuing lifelong learning is to learn something new every 90 days. I keep a Pendaflex file containing my schedule on how I intend to accomplish each new endeavor."

Starting a new job can be both exciting and intimidating, especially when you're coming to your new job from an entirely different industry. Such was the case for Joe DePreta, who left a film production company in New York City to work for BellSouth in Atlanta, Georgia. In high-technology organizations such as BellSouth, you have to learn the jargon and language before you can function at your full potential. This makes it incredibly important to master your company's most common nomenclature as quickly as you possibly can. DePreta found it particularly useful to make lists of difficult acronyms such as TDMA (time-division multiple access) in a spiral notebook. When he

arrived home at the end of each workday, DePreta would study his lists. First he memorized the acronyms and then read through a variety of textbooks and trade magazines to learn what they meant. DePreta's hard work paid off. "I've gotten good grades so far," he says. "And the reason is that, instead of reading *Rolling Stone,* I read wireless newsletters. I didn't allow myself the luxury of a grace period."

In many organizations, promotions and career growth are tied directly to employee education and learning. When Cincinnati, Ohio–based pharmaceutical-services company Omnicare created two new national sales-manager positions, Ron Welty was confident that he had one of the positions nailed. However, as many of us have already learned, there is no such thing as a sure thing—in life or in business. Omnicare's management decided to look outside the organization for job candidates, bypassing Welty and his coworkers. When Welty asked his boss why he was passed over for promotion, his boss told him the company wanted managers with M.B.A.'s. "They wanted someone with a shingle to appease Wall Street," says Welty. "I was shocked." However, instead of giving up, Welty decided that if he ever hoped to get ahead, he would have to work on improving his own skills and qualifications. He took the initiative to talk to his boss about the issue in depth and to closely review his own capabilities and long-term goals. As a result, Welty determined that he wasn't destined for a senior vice presidency at

(continued from previous page)

or charitable organizations. Get to know the people you're working with and helping.

8. Pick a successful role model at work and ask him or her to be your mentor.

9. Encourage—and participate in—team learning in the workplace.

10. Stay in touch with your spiritual side.

Make a Commitment to Learning

- Learn from mistakes.
- Ask others how they would have handled a situation that didn't turn out well.
- Be on the lookout for ways to increase your value to the organization.
- Don't wait for learning opportunities to be dropped in your lap; actively seek them out.
- Learn something new each and every day by talking to your coworkers about their jobs and how what they do relates to your job.

Omnicare unless he got his M.B.A. Rather than go through that particular ordeal—something Welty had no interest in doing at that point in his career—he took matters into his own hands and left for a position with Sparagowski & Associates, a small market-research company outside Toledo, Ohio. Within one year, Welty had doubled his top salary at Omnicare.

When Stewart Gray interviewed for a technical support position at Baudville, Inc., a paper products retailer located in Grand Rapids, Michigan, he knew that his work would be cut out for him. Although his background was primarily in the Microsoft Windows operating system environment, he would be expected to support Apple Macintosh applications as well. When he was hired, he took it upon himself to learn as much as he could by himself about how the Macintosh operates and, when he ran into a problem, to ask questions until he found a solution. However, once he got comfortable with his new position, Gray knew it was time to take the next step. "I tried to understand how my job was done in the past, so I could apply my own individual twist to the position. I had to distinguish myself from the others who had sat in this chair before me. Taking initiative was the only way. I tried to learn about all facets of the company, so that I could offer fresh solutions to old problems. Anyone can identify a problem; valuable employees can provide answers as well."

Kathy Knight, president and CEO of Baiglobal, a market research firm in Tarrytown, New York, is a big believer in the power of taking initiative, and she thinks employees

DECIDING YOUR CAREER'S WORK

BE YOUR OWN BOSS

Many people go from job to job and give little thought to their careers. In fact, most people spend more time and effort planning a vacation than they devote to planning their entire career. Here are some guidelines:

- **Consider what you enjoy doing.** One of the best places to start when considering your career is with those activities you most enjoy. Be specific. It's not good enough to say you want to "work with people," since more than 90 percent of all jobs will entail doing just that. When are you happiest? Most fulfilled? Most excited? These are the indicators that can help identify your life's work. Even if you are not the best at something you enjoy doing, you will likely improve as you spend time working at that activity.

- **What do other people tell you you're good at?** Feedback from your boss, coworkers, or even friends can be invaluable; it can help you see yourself as others see you. Don't dismiss those skills and attributes that come easily to you! These can indicate natural gifts that you may be able to parlay to your advantage.

- **Focus on developing your interests and skills.** Try to find a work environment that supports you and what you like to do by allowing you to use your natural skills. Many people spend time and energy fighting work circumstances they hate instead of further developing their natural skills and interests. If you are good at something, you have the chance to be great at it if you focus on it.

"I've come to the realization that the training needs in this country have flip-flopped in a short amount of time. The most pressing training need of front-line employees is in strategic management skills. And the basic training need of top managers is in basic communication skills."

—Kenneth H. Blanchard
Management Guru

shouldn't be afraid to take it. She is fond of telling the story of a worker who quickly rose within the organization. He did so by knowing what he wanted to do with his life and then doing what it took to achieve his goal. At work, this meant going "beyond the immediate boundary of tasks and anticipating what you probably meant but didn't articulate," according to Knight. "That's a godsend to any management." Although he initially paid the costs of his education to become a systems engineer, he soon realized that since all his training directly benefited his employer, the company should pay for it. He pressed the issue with management, and succeeded. Proud of the employee's initiative and persistence, Knight says, "He

TEN GREAT WAYS TO LEARN AT WORK

1. Shadow a coworker during his or her workday.

2. Accompany a salesperson on customer calls.

3. Attend a management staff meeting.

4. Meet top managers in your organization and volunteer to do assignments for them.

5. Go to a seminar on a new topic.

6. Develop a relationship with a mentor.

7. Fill in for another employee at a staff meeting.

8. Volunteer to join a team.

9. Volunteer for assignments that stretch your capabilities.

10. Gradually increase the scope of tasks assigned to you.

began to qualify himself before he came to management. There isn't a management in this world who wouldn't fall all over themselves for this kind of person."

Bert Minor of Carleton Place, Ontario, worked for Sweden-based IKEA, the world's largest furniture retailer, for the better part of five years. He recalls that one employee presented a particular management challenge. Says Minor, "Many of my employees believed that one coworker in the department was not right for the job. She would curse and get upset every time she believed a customer was taking advantage of the company. Of course these remarks were always made behind the scenes. This would happen many times in a day and many coworkers felt the woman would be better off in another department. I didn't agree. I knew she had potential and often told her so. I heard her in her dealings with customers both in person and on the phone. She was always very pleasant. I knew that if she could just start to understand her role from the perspective of the company and the customers she would be the best customer advocate in the department.

"After some time, I was forced to have a discussion with her. I explained that if ever one of her behind-the-scene outbursts was witnessed by a customer, she would be terminated. During our talk I explained that I knew she was in the right position . . . I knew that there was a 'customer-service guru' inside of her waiting to come out. All she had to do was to understand

> "To get ahead . . . learn from others with proven success and experience. Don't be afraid to adopt key parts of their styles."
>
> —Sharon Lipscomb, Special Assistant, U.S. Department of Justice

her role a bit more. I was able to convince her to start reading some of the books and articles in my service library." This was the beginning of a complete transformation for the employee. After reading the works of such business experts as Peter Drucker, Tom Peters, Lisa Ford, T. Scott Gross, and Ann Petit, the employee began to progressively change her attitude toward her job. She realized that only a very small percentage of IKEA's customers take advantage of certain situations. She saw issues from the customers' perspective and listened to their concerns and requests in a nonjudgmental way.

Says Minor, "After a few months she approached me and said, 'You know, reading those books made me finally understand what you have been saying all this time. Thanks. Do you think we could hold a meeting sometime after work and just talk about customer service and other important issues?' I told her that if she could get a few people to stay for a meeting, I would spring for pizza and would definitely stay after work. I was surprised when about ten coworkers stayed after work on their own time on a Sunday evening to discuss customer-service issues. I think a service library is a MUST and should be a part of every organization. These books not only enlighten coworkers but rejuvenate you when you start questioning your choice of careers."

During a discussion of ways to improve customer service, new Kentucky Housing Corporation (KHC) employees explained that

Your First 60 Days

When starting a new job, the first 60 days are critical in proving yourself to your employer. Linda Seale, head of the executive coaching firm Seale Group in New York City, suggests the following agenda for the first 60 days at work:

- **First 14 days: get to know four new people.** According to Seale, "Probably 95 percent of firings are the result of failing to fit into a company's culture. If people don't know you, they can't trust you." Set aside two days a week to have lunch with key people in your organization.
- **First 30 days: have a "How am I doing?" meeting with your boss.** Don't assume that your boss knows what you're doing. Says Seale, "It's not the boss's job to ask what you're working on and how it's going. It's up to you to seek out the boss."

(continued on next page)

they could not adequately describe any of the corporation's programs outside of their own areas of responsibility. Several seasoned employees also expressed their lack of familiarity with new and changing programs outside of their assigned areas. It was further discovered that many employees, both new and seasoned, were receiving little or no exposure to executive staff.

Due to quick, vast growth in both programs and staff, employees needed more information about the corporation than they were receiving from reading the corporate mission statements and in basic benefits orientation. In searching for solutions, one staff member described her orientation experience with a former employer that not only included benefits-related information but information about the overall organization as well. A consensus was then reached that providing an expanded orientation program periodically would be a wise investment to strengthen each employee's understanding of the corporation.

Orientation sessions, now typically a day and a half in length, are held quarterly for a small group of 20 to 25 new and seasoned employees. This is the first opportunity for some employees to participate in discussions with management. The chief executive officer initially sets the tone for the session by presenting the corporation's history and philosophy, followed by each chief officer's and department director's description of the programs they administer.

At the conclusion of the first day, each

(continued from previous page)

- **First 45 days: write your job description.** Once you've spent about a month and a half on the job, you should have a solid sense of your responsibilities. How do they differ from what you were led to expect? Write down your questions and review them with your boss. The goal: to create a real-world job description that you both agree on.

- **First 60 days: get something done.** Seale cautions against hastily assembling an agenda of easy-to-nail action items. While you must do something that will signal your potential to higher-ups, be careful to pick projects that make sense.

- **Next 60 days: reboot.** "Giving feedback, getting feedback, figuring out your place in the office—it's a continuous process. I'll be working on these things long after my 60 days are up."

> “Jump at opportunities to take on responsibilities. People should try new things—that's how to grow.”
>
> —KEVIN MURRAY, Deputy Director, Office of Information, U.S. Department of Agriculture

participating employee is asked to draw an assignment to report to the group at the follow-up session. For example, an employee from the operations staff might be assigned to locate a KHC underwriter and learn basic underwriting guidelines. Besides learning the practical applications throughout the corporation, the “KHC Scavenger Hunt” gives each participant the opportunity to network in other departments.

LIFE-LONG LEARNING

TAKE ACTION NOW!

1. Be a lifelong learner. You'll never know everything there is to know about your job. Make a point to learn something new every day.

2. Push your comfort zone. For example, have you always been afraid of speaking in front of others? Join Toastmasters International or take a class in stand-up comedy.

3. Spend some time in someone else's shoes. See what challenges your clients and coworkers face, and learn from them. Use your learning as a basis for improving your responsiveness to their needs.

4. Break out of your old paradigms. Look at your work from a new perspective. What would an outsider think about the way you do your job? Is it the best way?

5. Be flexible. Refuse to let your mind close itself off to new ideas and ways of doing business. Listen to what others have to say—*really* listen—and learn from their experience.

Developing Skills on the Job

While many organizations spend millions of dollars each year on formal training programs and reimbursements for formal employee education programs and schools, most employees still learn much of what they know on the job by observing others and by actually completing tasks and assignments themselves. As the old saying goes, "Tell me . . . I forget; show me . . . I remember; involve me . . . I understand." The key to developing skills on the job is to take advantage of every possible opportunity to learn a new skill. When it comes to building your skills, don't be shy. Identify the skills that you need, and then be assertive about getting them. Both you and your organization will benefit as a result of your efforts.

Build Your Skills:

- Identify problems and needs in your department.
- Match your skills to your department's problems and needs.
- Volunteer for projects and teams.
- Seek out others for advice.
- Connect with other departments and companies.

Joellyn Willis, an internal auditor for the Square D Company in Palatine, Illinois, was never one to be shy about using her expertise to help out other managers in need. To say the least, this made her very popular with her peers. Says Willis, "I got requests to help plants with projects, even when there weren't audits." It was just this willingness to help out, along with her business talent and high performance, that landed her a promotion to vice president of operations. She cautions those who want to follow in her footsteps not to neglect their current job

> “If you have initiative you can do anything—even if it means taking time to learn it.”
>
> —MIKE, from the Internet

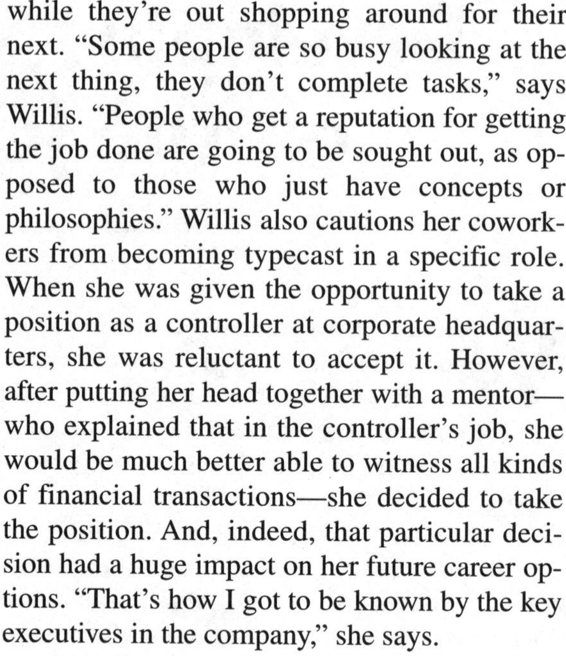

while they're out shopping around for their next. "Some people are so busy looking at the next thing, they don't complete tasks," says Willis. "People who get a reputation for getting the job done are going to be sought out, as opposed to those who just have concepts or philosophies." Willis also cautions her coworkers from becoming typecast in a specific role. When she was given the opportunity to take a position as a controller at corporate headquarters, she was reluctant to accept it. However, after putting her head together with a mentor—who explained that in the controller's job, she would be much better able to witness all kinds of financial transactions—she decided to take the position. And, indeed, that particular decision had a huge impact on her future career options. "That's how I got to be known by the key executives in the company," she says.

There are many different ways to become an expert in your chosen career. For Bernie Nagle, currently director of global business-process improvement for Berg Electronics in St. Louis, Missouri, the secret was to totally immerse himself in the art and science of analyzing and improving business processes. This required an incredible amount of initiative on his part, but it was the only way Nagle felt he would be able to achieve his career goal. Nagle did all the usual things: he took training classes in business-process improvement, he read books, and he joined associations dedicated to his chosen field. However, he went even further

than the norm by directly contacting authors of books he read and engaging them in conversations about the topic. He found most to be very open and interested in helping him. Says Nagle, "You can't be bashful, you can't expect people to come to you." As he became more and more knowledgeable about the topic of business-process improvement, he began writing articles in trade publications, and he even wrote a book on the topic: *Leveraging People and Profit: The Hard Work of Soft Management.*

Stelle Slootmaker worked as a proofreader for Printech Instant Ads in Grand Rapids, Michigan, a small ad design and printing house. When the owner asked her to proofread additional jobs, she said yes. When the owner asked Slootmaker if she could handle receptionist duties along with her proofreading, Slootmaker said yes, even though being a receptionist was not her cup of tea. When the owner asked her if she could write a brochure, she said yes again.

Slootmaker's career as a writer began. She had never written a brochure. In fact, she had never written much of anything professionally, except a few articles for a past employer's company newsletter. She didn't even know how to turn on a computer. A more honest answer might have been "I'll try" or "I think so." However, Slootmaker doubted that her boss would have given her the go-ahead on such a weak response. And her boss's request hadn't come out of the blue—Slootmaker had planted seeds, mentioning now and then that she'd like to write.

Five Ways to Improve Your Skills on the Job

1. Conduct an inventory of your skills and identify areas of weakness; make plans to address them.
2. Volunteer for assignments outside your assigned tasks.
3. Ask lots of questions.
4. Seek out and develop a relationship with a mentor.
5. Request opportunities to cross-train with coworkers—both inside and outside your department.

EXPRESSING YOUR OPPORTUNITY INTEREST

BE YOUR OWN BOSS

Most employees do not take initiative in making it clear to their manager what opportunities to learn and grow would interest them most at work. The better you can share your learning objectives, the better the chances you will have of achieving those expectations.

Opportunities on your current job. Most development occurs on the job, that is, in your present position at work. Make it clear what types of assignments would interest you and, better yet, volunteer for assignments that meet your development criteria when they arise. What tasks could you take over for your manager? Take the initiative to suggest projects that could improve your job and help you learn in the process. For example, offering to select software to make part of your job more efficient allows you the chance to learn about different software as well as the decisions that go into the selection process.

Opportunities within the organization. Be open to special assignments, cross-functional task forces, or chances to work with other groups in the organization. You can even help create such opportunities within the organization based on needs as they arise. Discuss career paths that are open to you if they are not readily apparent for your position. Volunteer to be the liaison to other departments for joint problems or to improve communication between the areas.

Formal learning opportunities. Make it clear what skills you would like to develop at work, or through training opportunities available in the organization, such as computer-based training or classes and seminars. Explore outside training opportunities through local colleges or other educational institutions. Ask to join one or more professional associations or attend a conference.

Her "just say yes" approach worked time and time again. Slootmaker said yes to newsletters, newspaper ads, and billboards. She nodded emphatically to editing technical treatises and rewriting corporate reports, always learning as she went along. Saying yes to an offer to write cover stories for a local trade magazine launched her freelance career. Says Slootmaker, "I remember slipping once and saying 'I think so.' I didn't get the job."

> "Today, in order to have job security, you've got to have a broader range of knowledge that enables you to handle a broader range of assignments and to work for more than one company."
>
> —Anthony P. St. John, Vice President for Human Resources, Daimler Chrysler Corp.

If employees aren't learning something new, then they aren't growing. And if they're not growing, then they're stuck—going nowhere. Not one to be stuck going nowhere, Karen Shorr, senior project coordinator for Universal Creative in Los Angeles, California, decided to take a risk and sign on for the Totally Nickelodeon Show, a new attraction at Universal Studios Hollywood. Says Shorr, "I wanted to be on that project because I'd never done a show before. I wanted to learn what it was like to bring a show to the park. That's how I pick projects. I ask, Is there something I will learn from it?" No doubt, Shorr, who previously worked only on rides and restaurants, has learned a lot in her new position. And that's just the way she likes it.

Looking for ways to make a positive impact on the youth in their community, a group of engineers at OKI America's Semiconductor Manufacturing plant in Tualatin, Oregon, took

the initiative to start and lead a technology club and to act as mentors to local students.

❝The more ideas you generate, the greater the odds a high-quality solution will result.❞

—Dr. Arthur VanGundy, *Idea Power*

When the personal computer industry was still in its infancy, and companies such as Apple Computer had only recently moved out of their founders' garages and into real office

CULTIVATING A MENTOR

Most people can use a professional coach in their career, someone they can learn from, ask advice of, or just use as a sounding board for plans and strategies. Such a person is often called a mentor. This person is typically older and further along in his or her career. A mentor doesn't work in your chain of command, although he or she may work in your organization. Here's some advice for finding a mentor:

■ **Seek someone you respect.** As you work with others in your organization, be on the lookout for those above you whose reputation and interactions are positive.

■ **Seek advice from potential mentors.** Ask to meet with individuals you admire for input on an idea or proposal you have. If a person is receptive to your inquiries, expand your discussions to advice about your career and related ambitions and plans. Ask the person who seems most amenable if he or she would serve as your mentor for career advice.

■ **Schedule periodic meetings.** Once you have selected a mentor, plan to connect at least once a quarter to discuss how things are going, questions or concerns you have about your job and career, and any related advice he or she might offer you.

space, few new hires had more than limited experience with this relatively new technology. Imagine for a moment how Susan Crocker, a 54-year-old ex–Peace Corps volunteer, must have felt when she reported to work her first day at Apple Computer and found an Apple II personal computer waiting for her at her desk. Working on a computer was a completely new experience for her. Crocker's first job at Apple was to document the product life cycle of the Apple II. There was only one problem: Crocker didn't have any idea what a product life cycle was.

She recalls, "We'd talk about R&D, manufacturing, marketing, and those were worlds that I simply was not familiar with. We didn't have models for marketing computers—there was nothing to follow. We were all learning." However, Crocker didn't give up—she kept at her job and began to catch on. In the process, she also learned how to manage her career. "I learned that in many respects, managing a career is like managing perpetual motion."

And learn it well she did. Within nine months, she was promoted to a marketing manager job. Five months later, she took on a role in strategic planning for marketing the Mac and Apple II. After the completion of that project, she jumped at the opportunity to become manager of the marketing communications department. "It was a lateral move, not a promotion, but it was the chance to learn something new and I grabbed it." Within a few more months, Crocker was selected to manage corporate communications for the entire company.

Skills Audit

1. Assess your current job. What skills could you learn to boost your job performance? What skills could you learn that would prepare you for advancement in your organization?

2. Develop a plan of action. Match skill needs to training opportunities, both inside and outside your organization. Schedule the training you need.

3. Present your plan to management. Make sure that your boss is aware of your training needs, and that he or she works with you to achieve your goals.

4. Make time for training. Don't consider training to be a burden; rather, look at it as a chance to expand your skills and your opportunities.

5. Scan the horizon. Your plan should be dynamic, not static. Keep current on changes in your job, technology, and your organization's business environment, and modify your plan when necessary to meet future needs.

Overcoming Obstacles

Every organization has its own set of limits and constraints. In some cases, these obstacles take the form of company policies or procedures. In other cases, they are embodied in people who feel more pride in stopping initiative than in facilitating it. And sometimes we bring our own emotional baggage with us to our jobs. Whatever the source, almost any obstacle can be overcome if you are simply willing to be persistent when you confront it. In life, you can choose to follow your dream, or you can choose to allow others to make you live *their* dreams. You can overcome the obstacles in your path, or you can allow them to stop you cold. Remember these words: *If it is to be, it begins with me.* The choice is yours. What path will you choose?

Adversity Builds Character

- Follow your own dream, not someone else's.
- Question limits and constraints.
- Ask "If it *were* possible . . ."
- Diffuse negative energy.
- Try a pilot project to test the waters.

We all face obstacles on the job. Some are easy to conquer, but others may seem as imposing as scaling the summit of Mount Everest. Brenda Lauderback, group president of Nine West Group, Inc., headquartered in White Plains, New York, tells the story of how she overcame almost insurmountable odds on her way up the corporate ladder of success.

"I learned a very valuable lesson early on in my career," Lauderback recounts. "I had just become a buyer in women's sportswear, which was one of my major career goals. There was a

SEEING CHALLENGES AS OPPORTUNITIES

BE YOUR OWN BOSS

With any problem, crisis, or mistake at work lies an opportunity for learning and growth. Those individuals who are able to consistently identify the opportunities in adversity are best able to learn and grow in their jobs and get ahead in their organizations.

Jump into problems as they arise. Develop a reputation for being a "take charge" person during times of adversity. Volunteer to explore the causes of the problems as they arise and potential solutions to fix those problems. Research the problem. Offer to chair a task force or conduct interviews or focus groups. Coordinate the identification of potential solutions, the analysis of the best solution, and the implementation of the preferred solution.

List the positives in any negative situation. Every negative situation has positive elements; be the one who points out the good news. Did you discover the problem instead of a customer? Would the problem have been worse if it had not been caught so soon? What can you learn from dealing with the situation that can help prevent a similar negative occurrence in the future?

Avoid naysayers. Individuals who are chronically negative or cynical can sap your energy and fuel your own negativity as well. Don't become a victim to the attitudes of those around you who never see the positive side of a situation. Avoid those individuals, or change the topic when it sounds like they are complaining for complaining's sake.

kind gentleman who owned a company I was doing business with. In his fatherly way, he congratulated me on my promotion and stated how young I was to be in such a position. We started talking, and I shared my ultimate (at that

> "A wise man will make more opportunity than he finds."
>
> —FRANCIS BACON

BALANCING WORK AND FAMILY

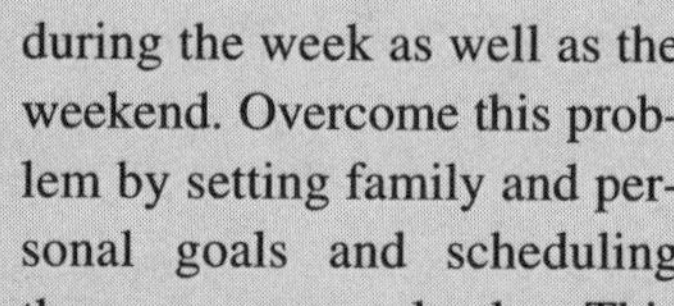

Ask anyone what is more important—work or family—and the answer will invariably be a resounding vote for family. However, work is also important to us, so we all have to find a balance between our work lives and our family lives. This is not an easy thing to do, but a sense of balance is important for you, your spouse, and your children.

Here are a few things you can do to make sure that your work life doesn't overwhelm your family life:

1. Set your priorities and work them into your schedule. If you have a demanding job, it can easily consume most of your waking hours during the week as well as the weekend. Overcome this problem by setting family and personal goals and scheduling them on your calendar. This can range from a visit to the zoo to playing a game of checkers or visiting a relative. If it gets scheduled, it's much more likely to happen than if left to chance or memory.

2. Make time to connect when you are with your family. Working a full-time schedule and taking care of the many details involved in running a household leave precious little time to connect with your kids and spouse. And if your work responsibilities require travel, you'll have even fewer opportunities to spend time with

> "If your employer sees your initiative, then all else will fall into place."
>
> —Maria, from the Internet

time) career goal with him, which was to be a vice president and general merchandise manager (GMM) in my company. He looked at me and said, 'Maybe you shouldn't set your goals too high. You will probably be disappointed. In the history of your company, there has never been a Jewish or female, much less black, vice

them. This means that you've got to make the time you have together count. If at all possible, avoid the urge to work late or spend weekends at the office. Set these times aside for you and your family to do things and to have fun together. Go to a movie, visit a museum, or take a short trip to the mountains or beach. If you tend to be constantly preempted by your work, be sure to reserve special dates when you will be at home, such as birthdays, anniversaries, holidays, and school breaks, or block out family time on your calendar to make sure it happens.

3. Build a network of support. When both parents work, schedules and responsibilities can easily conflict. In this situation, it is especially important that both partners pitch in to take care of the children's needs. Dropping the kids off at school, fixing them dinner, and reading them bedtime stories are *not* gender-specific activities! And for those times when work does consume you, be sure to build a network of friends and relatives who can give you perspective and balance and on occasion help care for the kids. You can also learn from your support group how others handle conflicting demands from work and family on their time.

So while it's easy to let your work life dictate your home and social life, it doesn't have to be the case. Taking the time to plan for priorities at work as well as home will help strengthen rather than weaken your family relationships. Make this investment of effort: you may very well find that you're one of the lucky ones who can balance work and family life.

president at GMM.' I said to him, 'In time, things will change, and I will be the first.'

"He was only trying to help, but I learned that no matter what the intention, never let anyone put limits on you. The only limitations you have are in your mind." Lauderback went on to become the first female, the first African

"Initiative drives us to make change, to build, to improve, to mobilize and lead."

—Joev, from the Internet

American, and the youngest person ever to become a vice president and general merchandise manager at Nine West.

Tips for Overcoming Obstacles Within Your Organization

- Learn to listen.
- Learn the background of your area.
- Learn the informal power network.
- Make time for the people as well as the task.
- Be sensitive to processes.
- Keep the right attitude and perspective.
- Use your resources to their fullest potential.

It's easy to consider obstacles on the job as negatives—problems that we have to conquer to find happiness on the job. However, if we change our perspective and look at obstacles from a slightly different angle, we'll see that they are often opportunities in disguise.

In the case of Kathy Harless, president of GTE Airfone, the Oak Brook, Illinois, company that provides phone service on airplanes, passenger trains, and other nontraditional locations, the process of overcoming obstacles on her job led to an incredible opportunity for growth in her career. According to Harless, "My professional turning point came in 1991 when I was asked to take on a special project to develop a process-reengineering model for GTE's Contact Center, where customers call to get phones installed or to make service changes. The goal was to redesign it to improve service and efficiency. In a very short time it became apparent to our team that this project was bigger and more complicated than anyone had anticipated. In addition to the customer-contact function, the whole process needed to be redesigned.

"One team grew into several teams, and in most cases these teams were headed by male managers. After months of meetings, gathering information, observing all aspects of our customer-contact process and looking at the best of the

best in other industries, we designed a completely new way of managing customer contact. It sounded great, except for one thing. Who was going to tell the boss that things weren't as great as he and many others thought? Somebody had to tell him that there was room for a lot of improvement. We also had to sell him on a new approach that would involve an up-front investment of millions of dollars."

> "Career advancement is much like marketing; your objective is to position yourself as the ideal solution to an organizational need."
>
> —J. Paul Costello, President, Costello, Erdlen & Company

Harless jumped at the opportunity to be the messenger. "The fact is, I wanted to do it. My team had done great work, I believed strongly in what we were proposing, and I wanted a shot at selling our ideas to the big guy—the president of all GTE Telephone Operations. He didn't like what he was hearing. But he listened to presentations from my team and others—all of which proposed radical, expensive, but necessary, solutions—and in the end, he approved the projects."

A few months later the GTE board of directors approved spending more than $1 billion to bring our plans to reality.

"It turned out to be a defining moment in my career. When I made that presentation I was an assistant vice president. Within six months I was the first woman vice president in the history of GTE Telephone Operations."

Today, it seems hard to imagine a time when women were not allowed to participate as full-fledged members of the New York Stock Exchange. However, until recently, they were not. It took the hard work of pioneers like

> “A winner is someone who recognizes his God-given talents, works his tail off to develop them into skills, and uses these skills to accomplish his goals.”
>
> —LARRY BIRD, Professional Basketball Coach/Player

Muriel Siebert and other determined women like her to knock down the walls that once held them back.

Siebert recalls her fight to get a seat on the Exchange. “I was brought up to believe in America as the land of opportunity. I had thought this included women. But as I moved upward in my profession and met more and more challenges, I found that this was not the case on Wall Street. To participate in a broad range of business activities, it was evident that I needed more than my partnership in a small Wall Street firm. I would have to buy a seat on the New York Stock Exchange. Nine of the first ten men that I asked to sponsor my membership turned me down. Then, the NYSE imposed a new condition. I was told that I needed a letter from a bank stating that it would lend me $300,000 of the then near-record $445,000 seat price. The banks said no until the NYSE would agree to admit me. It was a catch-22. It took me many months to find the right bank loans and sponsors, and on December 28, 1967, I was finally elected to membership. There were 1,365 men and me. And for ten years that's the way it stayed.”

Until only a few decades ago, cosmetics firms designed and targeted their products to Caucasians, leaving people of color, including African Americans and Asian Americans, to fend for themselves. Flori Roberts, founder of Flori Roberts Cosmetics, a division of Johnson Products Co., Inc., in Chicago, Illinois, changed

all that. Her small idea with big possibilities became an unqualified success, and it created an entirely new market niche. However, it wasn't easy starting her own business and taking on the big cosmetics firms. There were plenty of barriers and her success was never guaranteed.

Here is Roberts's story in her own words: "I remember precisely the day more than 30 years ago when my life was forever changed. I was producing a fashion show and I was listening to black models talk about their frustration at having to mix and match cosmetics designed for white skin tones. I could not believe that the big, sophisticated cosmetics industry had never catered to this part of the population. I realized that I had stumbled on a problem that others had never tried to solve, and I was determined to create cosmetics products that matched African American skin tones."

> "To be recognized at the workplace and to enhance your promotion chances, you must make things happen. You can be intelligent and inspirational, but intelligence and inspiration get exhibited through your initiatives."
>
> —NKOSINATHI, from the Internet

To achieve her dream, Roberts and her husband founded Flori Roberts, Inc., and tapped into a brand-new market of some 26 million people. Roberts continues, "When the customers lined up five-deep, the store owners became believers. The next turning point in my life came in the early 1980s, when I was told by doctors, 'You have skin cancer, and it's deep.' As a result of surgery to remove the malignancy, I was left with severe scars on my nose. I couldn't find any makeup, including my own, to really conceal them. I soon realized that many people face the same dilemma daily when their ordinary makeup rubs off and their scars or birthmarks are revealed. This awakening inspired me to create a new line—Dermablend

> “Initiative means being able to reason out problems and complete tasks successfully with little supervision. It is a definite plus and will be noticed.”
>
> —Anonymous from the Internet

Corrective Cosmetics. It's camouflage makeup designed to conceal skin flaws and discoloration of all skin tones."

"I'm the last person who would have ever predicted that my future would include serving as president and CEO of an international tool manufacturing company," says Nancy Sanders Peterson, who became president and CEO of Peterson Tool Company, Inc., not as a result of career planning but through the tragic death of her husband, John Peterson, five weeks after he learned he had cancer. According to Peterson, "At the funeral I looked at my six children and all of the families of John's employees, and I realized I had to not only do what John said and take over the business, but I had the responsibility and the duty to make it work, no matter what.

"I decided not to tell existing clients about John's death for six months, feeling that they would have little comfort with tooling produced under the direction of an unproven homemaker in a male-dominated industry. I also inherited a disciplined, highly professional cadre of seasoned employees, strong on loyalty. We worked as a team, filling orders, meeting production schedules, and shortening delivery times. At the end of six months, with orders delivered early and to specification, I paid personal visits to clients, thanking them for their business. By then, I had a proven track record. I didn't lose one client."

Under Peterson's leadership, the company's

staff has grown from just 24 to 125 employees. Sales have increased steadily every year, the company has diversified its client base, and it has expanded successfully into international markets. Says Peterson, "As my experience taught me, in the business world risk and opportunity go hand in hand. If you believe in yourself and aren't afraid to take calculated risks, you can create wonderful opportunities."

STRATEGIES FOR TAKING INITIATIVE

1. Break large tasks into smaller pieces. It's a lot easier to achieve many small goals than it is to achieve one large goal.

2. Believe in yourself. Others can't put limits on you if you don't let them.

3. Maintain a positive attitude. The right attitude is 90 percent of the solution.

4. Get in the habit of overcoming obstacles. The more obstacles you overcome, the more momentum you generate to carry you over the next one.

5. Review lessons learned. Take time to assess how you overcame an obstacle, and how you could do an even better job at it the next time.

Career Options

The traditional notion of career—a job or series of closely related jobs that we hold during our entire working lives—has undergone a major change over the past decade. Today, a career is all about having options. More than ever before, workers are finding their dream jobs by telecommuting, job sharing, pursuing multiple careers, and starting their own businesses. Work is increasingly becoming a state of mind more than a place to go. With the advent of computers, cellular phones, fax machines, and other technological advances in the workplace, there's no reason why you can't pursue the career you want, when and where you want it. Consider the following stories of individuals who exploited their career opportunities. Perhaps you'll soon be joining them.

There Are No Limits

- Identify options for your ideal work.
- Seek out role models from other organizations; try to find someone who is doing what you want to do.
- Propose your job alternative to management.
- Have a backup plan.
- If you are initially discouraged, persist and revisit your alternatives.

When a young, idealistic IBM programmer named Jay Elliot heard Tom Watson, Jr.—the powerful chairman of the company—testify before the Senate Foreign Relations Committee that America's war effort in Vietnam was poorly managed, Elliot felt compelled to react. Elliot wrote Watson a letter that said in part, "If you think Vietnam is being run poorly, how about your own company?" Accompanying the letter were 20 pages of detailed suggestions for improvement, touching every part of the mammoth organization. Two weeks later, Elliot was summoned by Watson to join him for a cup of coffee. However, instead of firing

Elliot, Watson told him how thrilled he was that Elliot had the guts to write his letter, and to take the time to make so many insightful suggestions. Elliot was immediately sent to the company's headquarters in Armonk, New York, to talk to IBM's corporate planning staff, and to begin an entirely new career path within the company. For the duration of his career at IBM, Elliot led a charmed life, catapulting past all his peers as he rose through the company ranks.

> "A man is not finished when he's defeated; he's finished when he quits."
>
> —Richard M. Nixon

As director of government and community affairs at BankBoston headquarters in Boston, Massachusetts, Grady Hedgespeth was concerned that area investment banks were not effectively serving low-to-moderate-income communities. To address this ongoing issue, Hedgespeth proposed formation of the First Community Bank, and he wrote a strategy document and submitted it to management.

Management approved, establishing the BankBoston Development Company and naming Hedgespeth president. The organization planned to pump more than $100 million into target communities in Massachusetts, Connecticut, Rhode Island, New Hampshire, and parts of Florida within its first four years of existence in the form of affordable-housing development loans, traditional loans, and small-business equity investments. Says Hedgespeth, "This will be a powerful engine for economic growth. In a nutshell, we're trying to take our expertise and bring it to the communities that may not have fully

benefited from it before." And all thanks to Hedgespeth's original idea, and a bit of initiative.

William Thompson clearly understands that the only way you can be sure that you'll achieve your dreams is to go after them. Before starting Boston-based Summit Group, Inc., a multifaceted shell organization that includes a number of fast-food franchises, an engineering services firm, and a company that does computer systems integration, Thompson was an Eagle Scout, an honor student, a star athlete, and the first African American from South Carolina to receive an appointment to the U.S. Air Force Academy.

After a stint in the air force as a pilot and a move to Delta Airlines, he started Summit Group, a tax-planning firm. As a result of a very successful real estate investment made with a group of clients, the company gained a sizable cash windfall. According to Thompson, this windfall "gave me the cash to do other things." These other things include the fast-food businesses, the engineering services firm, and the computer systems integration company. With combined gross revenues of approximately $3.7 million last year, Thompson's companies are successful—and so is Thompson.

So what drives him? "I had the goal of owning a Mercedes 450SL with a phone. This was back when not everybody had a car phone." Once he got his car phone (and the nice ride that came along with it), he set his sights on building a $1 million cash account in his bank.

Effective Career Strategies

In his book *The Top 10 Career Strategies,* Gary Joseph Grappo, founder and former president of CareerEdge career seminars, explains his blueprint for success:

1. Update your attitude.
2. Discover the future growth industries.
3. Develop the right skills.
4. Learn to sell yourself like a company sells a product.
5. Build a network.
6. Change jobs frequently.
7. Act as an independent contractor.
8. Think national.
9. Go global.
10. Start your own business.

It's probably no surprise that he accomplished that goal, too. "I'm a firm believer that there's not much I can't accomplish if I want to," says

CONSTANTLY SEARCH FOR YOUR NEXT JOB

BE YOUR OWN BOSS

There's an old saying that the time to start looking for a new job is the day you take your current job. Such an attitude keeps you fresh and helps you to avoid being overly reliant on your existing position. By constantly being on the lookout for new opportunities both within the organization and outside it, you remain in control of your future. Identifying opportunities you could fill helps to build your confidence—even if you stay in your existing position. Alternatives always give you freedom, even if you do not use them.

Examine the career-path potential of your current position. Have others who held your job been promoted, or did they leave the organization? How long did they stay in your position? Although not fail-safe, looking at what became of your predecessors provides a helpful perspective on the likely scenarios for your own advancement.

Identify skills you will need to move ahead. Determine what skills and qualifications are necessary to reach your career goals. Set out to obtain as many of those skills and qualifications in your current position as you can, even to the point of making them a part of your job responsibilities.

Make the most of your current position. Things change. You never know how long you will be in your current position, so do all you can to get the most out of it. Learn the job processes and skills in your area, develop contacts throughout the organization, and determine if the type of work and industry fit who you are and what you want to do with your life.

> ❝I've created my own positions, jobs, and myself. 'Preparation' for me was the key . . . my ability to research, focus, initiate, plan, and communicate, orally and in writing. I went from working as a seventh-grade teacher to being a director of fundraising. It took three years of 'preparation.'❞
>
> —CATHARINE COOK, Director of Development, Center for Applied Technology

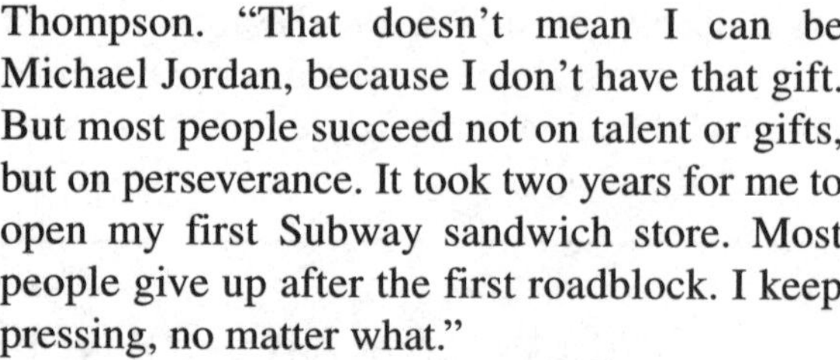

Thompson. "That doesn't mean I can be Michael Jordan, because I don't have that gift. But most people succeed not on talent or gifts, but on perseverance. It took two years for me to open my first Subway sandwich store. Most people give up after the first roadblock. I keep pressing, no matter what."

None of us knows everything there is to know about our jobs—there is always room to learn something new and valuable. Sometimes, however, this learning may be in areas that aren't directly related to our work. Because of that, you never know what new paths your learning may lead you down. Charlotte Clarke, then a process engineer for Stamford, Connecticut–based office equipment manufacturer Pitney Bowes, was looking for ways to improve her job performance and long-term career prospects when, several years ago, she enrolled in acting classes. Why? Clarke says, "I thought it would help me in my corporate life. I tend to be somewhat introverted. I thought this would bring me out, help with my presentation skills and communicating with strangers." She also had a low-key modeling career. When her job was eliminated in 1996, she started looking for a new job within the company while also taking time to dust off her modeling portfolio. Before long, she landed several modeling jobs. "It really helped me deal with the stress and uncertainty of my job," she says. Not only that, but it paid the bills and ended up getting her face plastered across local city buses

and on a billboard around the corner from Pitney Bowes. So why does Clarke do it? "I'm an engineer. My job at Pitney Bowes is in no way impacted by my modeling. There is some financial benefit to it, but that's not why I do it. Most people in corporate America play golf or tennis. I do this for the same reason—because I like it."

Besides running a busy Kentucky Fried Chicken fast-food restaurant in Boulder, Colorado, Danny Wagner has embarked on a new vocation: illustrating children's books. When he learned that a local fifth grader was writing a book for publication, Wagner gave him a portfolio of illustrations to review. The young writer liked what he saw, and the pair teamed up to complete the book. Wagner and his partner are looking forward to the book's publication, and they are planning a book-signing party at Wagner's KFC restaurant to kick off sales.

As an administrative assistant to two managers of the Hewitt Investment Group (HIG) division of Hewitt Associates LLC, in Lincolnshire, Illinois, Ellen Peckler was in a rut. She wanted more responsibility and craved a creative outlet, since much of her time was spent typing statistics. At the same time, group morale was low and associates were feeling disconnected from management and from one another. Peckler's bosses, John Allen and Gautam Dhingra, challenged Peckler to find a solution

> "Initiative is important for three reasons:
>
> 1. The most productive workplace is one where everyone is proactive. Initiative implies that you are willing to take responsibility and do your share.
> 2. Anyone can perform everyday, run-of-the-mill tasks, but the difference between successful businesses and others is the ability to meet challenges creatively. People with initiative perform day-to-day tasks with more energy, too.
> 3. Initiative is positive for personal career development because it shows you comprehend problems and challenges, have the skills to meet them, and are motivated enough to act!"
>
> —Debbie, from the Internet

> “If you find the job you really dream of and want to succeed, initiative is definitely what you need to start your success.”
>
> —JENNIFER, from the Internet

to both problems. They appointed Peckler "associate relations coordinator" and turned her loose. Here's what happened:

- Peckler conducted one-on-one interviews with associates in Lincolnshire and asked questions that she devised, such as "What other interests do you have that you would like to see incorporated into your role?" and "What would you like to tell management anonymously?"

- Peckler organized a meeting with her organization's five managers to discuss interview

SIMPLIFYING YOUR LIFE

Sometimes taking initiative means making changes that will enhance your life both at work and away from the office. Here are six tips for simplifying your life from simplicity guru Elaine St. James, author of *Simplify Your Life: 100 Ways to Slow Down and Enjoy the Things That Really Matter:*

1. Resign from any organizations whose meetings you dread.

2. Learn to live with less information. Stop watching TV news. Cancel half your magazine subscriptions.

3. Work where you live, or live where you work.

4. Be in bed by 9:00 P.M. one night a week.

5. Live on half of what you earn, and save the other half.

6. Keep asking, "Is this going to simplify my life?"

issues and to brainstorm ways to better communicate with associates. With the channels of communication open, she needed a way to bring the HIG together and incorporate some much-needed humor. Initiative struck, and Peckler created a monthly newsletter called *First Friday.* The first issue included results from a survey on job fulfillment. The second featured an interview with the organization's director in which he answered some tough questions about managing the group.

> "If you have a willingness or interest in what you're pursuing, then the desire to be the best you can be at it will come to you. You can learn the rest."
>
> —CATHERINE, from the Internet

- After being asked by her manager to roll out *First Friday* on a nationwide basis, initiative struck again. Peckler sent out biography forms to all associates with questions about employee hometowns, nicknames, specialties, and more. She then typed up the responses and distributed the document, *Cast of Characters,* to each associate before the June newsletter. This action improved employee communication and morale.

- Peckler approached her bosses with a new idea: recognizing associate anniversaries. Using clip art and the company duplicating center, she designed anniversary cards to send to associates on their anniversaries with HIG. Associates proudly display their anniversary cards on their computers and bookshelves, and Peckler has the satisfaction of being creative while helping others.

- Peckler came up with the idea of a biannual Staff Appreciation Day. On this day, associ-

ates find treats and surprises on their desks, play games, eat lunch together (something they're not always able to do), and participate in a hilarious white elephant auction.

- To celebrate her boss's 20 years of service to Hewitt, Peckler is planning a roast toast where associates are invited to contribute warm and humorous memories. In the words of a very busy Ellen Peckler, "It should be a hoot!"

When Cindy Casselman first accepted a position in corporate communications for Xerox Corporation in Stamford, Connecticut, she had her work cut out for her. Rather than getting their company news from internal sources, most of the organization's 85,000 employees found out what was going on by reading their daily newspaper. Casselman was determined to change that. "Employees were telling us they wanted timely, relevant, honest information. They wanted the truth, with no corporate spin. They wanted to know where they stood and where the company stood."

She put together a modest budget and assembled a team of employee volunteers, dubbed the Sanctioned Covert Operation (SCO). Because of her efforts, and those of the rest of the team, employees can read the latest company news and discuss and debate company issues on WebBoard, the company's intranet site. As a result, employees communicate better

Career Moves

In her book *Who's Running Your Career?,* Caela Farren presents the Capability Portfolio, a model for anyone who wants to explore his or her career options:

- Catching the drift of emerging trends and needs in society, technology, and industry
- Anticipating new niches, products, or services that meet those needs
- Proposing realistic options and solutions
- Analyzing the benefits to organizations, industries, customers, and the bottom line
- Bolstering your case with prior accomplishments, competencies, and service role experience
- Leveraging your reputation in your profession, industry, and organization
- Engaging your services in accord with your desired compensation, preferred employment package, and environmental needs

and are more connected throughout the organization, and morale has improved. Not only that, but the success of WebBoard landed Casselman a promotion to executive assistant to the head of corporate research and technology. "The WebBoard raised my profile and proved that I could follow through on an ambitious project and form the relationships needed to support the project. It definitely helped me win my new job."

Many of us don't consider all the career options available to us until a firing, layoff, downsizing, or the imminent threat of some adversity forces us to evaluate our status. After years of looking, and after many rejections, Gregg Ketter, a construction worker, finally landed a job with KCOP Channel 13 in Los Angeles, California. Unfortunately, as a result of extensive cost cutting and resultant layoffs of personnel at KCOP, Ketter was back on a construction site within a year. Instead of giving up his dream, Ketter got right back to work finding a job in television. Eventually, he was hired by KTTV Fox 11 News, also in Los Angeles as the weekend weatherman. But this time, after the celebration was over, Ketter decided that there had to be a way to avoid depending on the far-from-secure television entertainment business to provide him with job security and a steady income.

His solution was to give motivational speeches. At first, he volunteered to speak, but he was slowly able to charge a fee for his talks,

Making A Move?

Are you thinking about pulling up roots and moving someplace new? Consider these factors before you make a final decision on where to go:

1. Size of the community and access to schools, stores, your workplace, and other essentials
2. Quality of life
3. Overall personality of the residents
4. Weather
5. Job opportunities
6. Cultural events and venues
7. Availability of attractive, affordable housing

> “If you want to succeed in your career, you have to get off your bum and work hard to achieve your goals! You can have all the brains in the world, but if you don't put them to some use they won't help you at all. Initiative is the path to success—hard work will be rewarded.”
>
> —Bronwyn, from the Internet

and he landed bigger and better clients. Today, his roster includes such top-flight organizations as Citibank, McDonald's, and IBM. Ketter has increased not only his job options but also his income and his job security—and he is having a wonderful time doing what he loves. “I love giving people good news; there's just so much bad out there. Working a couple of jobs is normal for me. I've inherited my father's work ethic.”

If you don't make your career decisions for yourself, you can be sure that someone else will make them for you. However, you're the only person who knows exactly what your best interests are. Tawny Halbert worked on the team that created the Dante's Peak attraction at Universal Studios Hollywood Theme Park. After her work on that project was finished, Halbert faced a decision: should she cast her lot with the sure-to-be-popular Terminator 2 exhibit, or should she go for the much less glamorous buffet restaurant project? While each had its good points and bad, she eventually settled on the restaurant: at only one year, the project would be much shorter in duration than the three years or so required to take on the Terminator 2 exhibit, giving her much greater flexibility in the long run. Says Halbert, “I like shorter projects. Being out on the site and dealing with people is more rewarding than sitting in my cubicle doing paperwork. Plus, shorter projects leave you open to more opportunities.

UNLIMITED OPPORTUNITY

TAKE ACTION NOW!

1. Take charge of your career. Ultimately, you are the one who decides what work you're going to do, and what jobs you're going to accept.

2. Listen to your heart. Do what *you* want to do—not what *others* want you to do.

3. Do what you love. If you're doing the work that gives you the most personal satisfaction and meaning, then everything else will work out.

4. Don't limit your options. Do and learn things that give you more options for the future in your career, not fewer.

5. Have a plan. Putting together a plan for achieving your career goals will vastly increase the odds that you will accomplish them.

It's hard to be on a three-year project and watch all these other opportunities pass you by."

When you work in a well-established position within a well-established firm, it's easy to become complacent about your career progression or job ladder. For Michael Cyr, who had been a manufacturing technician at Hewlett-Packard for 18 years, it came down to deciding whether to take the safe, well-trodden path of clear assignments and unambiguous responsibilities, or travel the path less taken—one that was undefined and potentially far less stable. Fortunately, HP's management encouraged Cyr's initiative and allowed it to blossom. Says

> "Initiative is ambition. You accomplish, achieve, accept, accommodate, accumulate, absorb, adapt, adjust, affect, amuse, amend, analyze, apply, appoint, appreciate, approach—all of which cannot be done without initiative."
>
> —NOVELIDEA, from the Internet

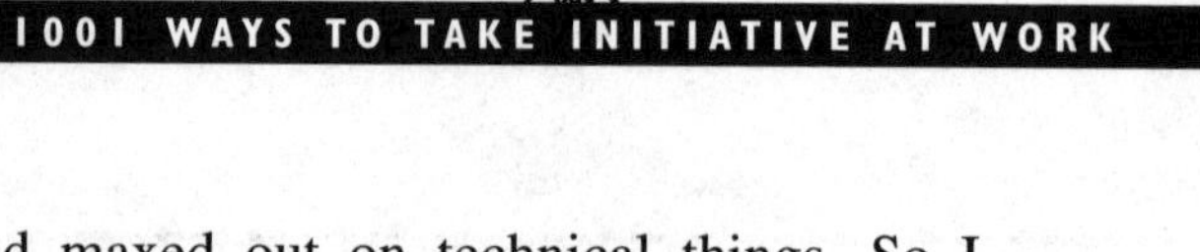

Cyr, "I had maxed out on technical things. So I looked at myself, looked around the company, and started doing what I wanted to do. Sometimes I think, What have I gotten myself into? But I'm inspired. I just need to manage my projects so I don't burn out." As a result of taking a chance and letting his heart guide him, Cyr has achieved his wildest career dreams. Instead of doing the same job over and over again, he now has the freedom to work on projects that really interest him—from plant-safety initiatives, to Intranet design.

GOOD ENOUGH ISN'T GOOD ENOUGH

My child, beware of "good enough,"
It isn't made of sterling stuff;
It's something anyone can do,
It marks the many from the few.

"Good enough" has no merit to the eye,
It's something anyone can buy,
Its name is but a sham and bluff,
For it is never "good enough."
The flaw which may escape the eye
And temporarily get by,
Shall weaken underneath the strain
And wreck the ship or car or plane.

With "good enough" the shirkers stop
In every factory and shop;
With "good enough" the failures rest
And lose to one who gives the best.

With "good enough" have ships been wrecked,
The forward march of armies checked,
Great buildings burned and fortunes lost;
Nor can the world compute the cost
In life and money it has paid
Because at "good enough" one stayed.
Who stops at "good enough" shall find
Success has left them far behind.

For this is true of you and stuff
Only the best is "good enough."
—Edgar A. Guest

APPENDIXES

Appendix I

Index to Innovators

Q

R

S

T

U

Appendix II

Index to Featured Companies

Bread Loaf Construction Company, 97
Middlebury, VT
Construction

Cerdec Corporation, 59
Washington, PA
Pigments and colorants

Cheeseborough Ponds, 44
Greenwich, CT
Home and personal care products

Child Nutrition Research Committee, 130
Sacramento, CA
Government agency

Children's Medical Center, 31
Dallas, TX
Health care

Citicorp/Citibank, 107
New York, NY
Financial services

City of Carrollton, 31
Carrollton, TX
City government

City of Chandler, 34
Chandler, AZ
City government

City of Longview, 31
Longview, TX
City government

City of New York, 53
Department of Parks & Recreation
New York, NY
City government

City of New York, 55
Sanitation Department
New York, NY
City government

City Public Service, 39
San Antonio, TX
Gas and utilities

CLEAR Communications, 28
New Zealand
Telecommunication systems

Clorox Company, 35
Oakland, CA
Household products

Communicorp, 134
Ft. Lauderdale, FL
Direct marketing

Conley McDonald LLP, 99
Brookfield, WI
Accounting services

Conoco Oil, Inc., 55
Ponca City, OK
Refinery

Copeland Corporation, 24
Sidney, OH
Air-conditioning and refrigeration

Corona Norco Unified School District, 130
Corona, CA
Education

The Coronation, 110
Bowmanville, Ontario, Canada
Restaurant

CP Corporation, 101
San Jose, CA
Printing, mailing, fulfillment, and turnkey manufacturing

Crystal Gateway, 140
Marriott Hotels
Arlington, VA
Hospitality

Dana Corporation, 14, 58
Elizabethtown, KY
Automotive industry supplier

Delco-Remy, Inc., 121
Flint, MI
Automotive industry supplier

Delta Airlines, 206
Atlanta, GA
Air transportation

Digital Equipment Corporation, 159
Maynard, MA
Computers

Disneyland, 64
Anaheim, CA
Entertainment

Domino's Pizza, 142
Ann Arbor, MI
Restaurants

Dow Corning Inc., 79
Midland, MI
Plastics/powders/resins

Esprit de Corp, 67, 150
San Francisco, CA
Clothing

Fastenal, Inc., 29
Winona, MN
Nuts, bolts, and fasteners

First National Bank of Chicago, 117
Chicago, IL
Banking

Fleet Financial Group, 94
New York, NY
Financial planning

Flori Roberts Cosmetics, Inc., 200
Chicago, IL
Cosmetics

FMC Corporation, 150
Chicago, IL
Heavy equipment

Foote Cone & Belding, 150
Chicago, IL
Ad agency

Ford Motor Company, 101,124
Wilson, MI
Automobiles and trucks

Fotozines, 5
Chicago, IL
Photo services

Four Seasons Hotel, 134
Toronto, Ontario, Canada
Hospitality

Gap Inc., 16, 80, 86
San Francisco, CA
Retail clothing

Gardner Merchant, 12
Kenley, Surrey, UK
Catering

Gateway Computer, 133
San Diego, CA
Computers

GE Medical Systems, 71
Milwaukee, WI
Medical devices

General Electric Transportation Services Division, 64
Erie, PA
Locomotives

General Motors, Inc., 121, 131
Detroit, MI
Automobiles and trucks

Georgia Common Access Team, 121
Atlanta, GA
State government

Georgia-Pacific Corporation, 123
Atlanta, GA
Building materials

GGS Information Services, 61
York, PA
Information technology

Going Places, 13, 97
Woking, Surrey, UK
Travel agency

GTE Airfone, 198
Oak Brook, IL
Wireless telephone technology

GTE-Sylvania, 83
Division of GTE Corporation
Irving, TX
Electronics

Guest Quarters Suites Hotel, 137
Doubletree Inc.
Boston, MA
Hospitality

Harza Engineering, 22
Chicago, IL
Engineering and environmental consulting

Hewitt Associates, LLC, 209
Lincolnshire, England, UK
Management consulting, employee benefits

Hewlett-Packard, Inc., 66, 91, 166, 215
Palo Alto, CA
Computer products, services, and support

Hitachi, Inc., 63
Tokyo, Japan
Electronics

Home Depot, 33, 131
Atlanta, GA
Hardware and building supplies

IBM Almaden Research Center, 80
San Jose, CA
Research

IBM alphaWorks, 42
San Jose, CA
Internet technology research

IBM Corporation, 76, 204
Armonk, NY
Computers

IKEA, 183
Almhult, Sweden
Retail furniture

Illinois Power Co., 38
Decatur, IL
Public utility

Industrial Edge USA, 135
Orange, NJ
Apartment house supplier

Ink&Air, 165
Norwood, MA
Public relations

IntroKnocks, 125
New York, NY
Business-to-business greeting cards

Italianni's, 137
Plymouth, MN
Restaurant

iVillage, 172
New York, NY
Virtual site

Jayson Home & Garden, 34
Chicago, IL
Florist and garden center

The Nature Company, 139
Berkeley, CA
Environmentally friendly gifts

Net Daemons Associates, Inc., 106
Woburn, MA
Computer networking

Nine West Group, Inc., 194
White Plains, NY
Women's footwear and accessories

Northern Telecom, 60
St. John, New Brunswick, Canada
Telephone services

OKI America, 191
Tualatin, OR
Semiconductors

Omnicare, 179
Cincinnati, OH
Pharmaceutical services

Oregon Saw Chain, 12
Portland, OR
Chain saws

Oticon, 36
Hellerup, Denmark
Hearing aid manufacturer

Peterson Tool Company, Inc., 202
Nashville, TN
Cutting tools

Phoenix Children's Hospital, 177
Phoenix, AZ
Health care

Pinnacle Brands, 42
Grand Prairie, TX
Sports trading cards

Pitney-Bowes Inc., 208
Stamford, CT
Copying and duplicating machines and supplies

PNC Bank, 20
Pittsburgh, PA
Banking

Pontiac Division, General Motors, Inc., 131
Detroit, MI
Automobiles

Printech Instant Ads, 189
Grand Rapids, MI
Graphic advertising

Private Bank of BankBoston, 83
Stamford, CT
Banking

Quantum Computer Services, 36
(now America Online)
Sterling, VA
Internet service provider

Right Management Consultants, 20
Philadelphia, PA
Consulting

Ruby Tuesday, 141
Greenville, SC
Restaurant

San Diego Housing Commission, 34
San Diego, CA
City government agency

Schwartz Communications, 155
Waltham, MS
Communications

Sears Licensed Businesses Unit, 81
Chicago, IL
Franchise licensing

Second Harvest, 43
Chicago, IL
Food bank network

Sergeant's Program, 165
Washington, DC
Business training

Sikorsky Aircraft, 90
Stratford, CT
Military, industrial, and commercial helicopters

SmithKline Beecham, 94
Philadelphia, PA
Pharmaceuticals

Southwest Airlines, 136
Dallas, TX
Air transportation

Square D Company, 187
Palatine, IL
Wiring devices

SSM Health Care, 89
St. Louis, MO
Health care

St. Mary's Health Center, 114
St. Louis, MO
Health care

Starbucks Coffee, 7, 134
Seattle, WA
Retail coffee houses

State of Massachusetts, 26
Boston, MA
State government

Stew Leonard's, 130, 144
Norwalk, CT
Grocery and deli

Strategic Innovations, Inc., 167
Valparaiso, IN
Computer system design and connecting

Summit Group, Inc., 206
Boston, MA
Financial services

Syncrude Canada, Ltd., 56
Fort McMurray, Alberta, Canada
crude oil supplier

Tandy Corporation, 45, 67
Ft. Worth, TX
Electronics

Tennant Corporation, 122
Minneapolis, MN
Construction machinery and equipment

Tennessee Valley Authority, 115
Knoxville, TN
Federal government agency

Tom & Sally's Handmade Chocolates, Inc., 10
Brattleboro, VT
Chocolatier

Toronto Transit Commission's Surface Operations Training Center, 45
Toronto, Canada
Public transportation

Trefethen Winery, 22
Napa, CA
Winery

Tripod, 159
Williamstown, MA
Internet services

Tri-United Companies, 151
Skokie, IL
Real estate

UNICEF, 150
New York, NY
Charitable organization

United Airlines, 120
Chicago, IL
Air transportation

United Electric Controls, 4, 11, 43, 55, 70, 109
Watertown, MA
Hermetically sealed switches, electrical controls

Universal Creative, 191
Universal City, CA
Entertainment

Universal Studios, 214
Universal City, CA
Entertainment

University Hospital, 162
Denver, CO
Health care

University of Delaware, 58
Newark, DE
Education

University of Victoria, 98
Victoria, British Columbia, Canada
Education

US Airways, 33
Winston-Salem, NC
Air transportation

U.S. Postal Service, 140
Washington, DC
Mail delivery

USWest Communications, 5
Chicago, IL
Cellular telephone services

Varian Ion Implant Systems, 157
Gloucester, MA
Electronic equipment and supplies

Walt Disney World, 136
Orlando, FL
Entertainment

Wang Laboratories, 162
Billerica, MA
Computer peripherals and software

Western Resources, 82
Topeka, KS
Public utility

Wittman-Hart, Inc., 43, 53
Peoria, IL
Information technology consultant

Work/Family Directions, Inc., 166
Boston, MA
Consulting

Xaloy, Inc., 78, 95
Pulaski, VA
Bimetallic cylinders

XEL Communications, 123
Aurora, CO
Telephone equipment and systems

Xerox Corporation, 69, 163, 212
Stamford, CT
Photocopiers and computer peripherals

Ziff-Davis Publishing Company, 154
New York, NY
Publishing

ABOUT BOB NELSON

Bob Nelson is president of Nelson Motivation, Inc. He is the author of 18 books on business and management, including *1001 Ways to Reward Employees, 1001 Ways to Energize Employees, Managing for Dummies, Consulting for Dummies, Motivating Today's Employees,* and *Empowering Employees Through Delegation,* as well as *365 Ways to Manage Better Page-A-Day® Perpetual.* He holds an MBA from the University of California at Berkeley and is a doctoral candidate in the Executive Management Program of The Peter F. Drucker Graduate Management Center of The Claremont Graduate School in Los Angeles. He lives in San Diego.

Mr. Nelson is publisher of a monthly newsletter, *Rewarding Employees,* and has created a variety of additional products including videos, audios, software, learning tools and more to help put concepts from his books into practice. For information about his newsletter and available products or to schedule Mr. Nelson or one of his associates to consult or present to your company, association, or conference, contact:

1-800-575-5521
Nelson Motivation, Inc.
P.O. Box 500872
San Diego, CA 92150-9973
619-673-0690/619-673-9031 (fax)
E-mail: BobRewards@aol.com
Website: www.nelson-motivation.com

NOTES

COMMENTS/CORRECTIONS/ADDITIONS

This book is updated each printing. If you have any comments, corrections or additions, please send them to the address below:

Nelson Motivation, Inc.
P.O. Box 500872
San Diego, CA 92150-9973

If you know of an exceptional way to motivate employees or have a suggestion or story that you'd like included in a subsequent edition of this book, please forward it with contact information to the above address.

NOTES

NOTES

NOTES

NOTES

NOTES

NOTES

NOTES